Customer Loyalty

A guide for time travelers

Dr Sionade Robinson and Lyn Etherington

© Dr Sionade Robinson and Lyn Etherington 2006

All rights reserved. No reproduction, copy or transmission of this
publication may be made without written permission.

No paragraph of this publication may be reproduced, copied or transmitted
save with written permission or in accordance with the provisions of the
Copyright, Designs and Patents Act 1988, or under the terms of any licence
permitting limited copying issued by the Copyright Licensing Agency, 90
Tottenham Court Road, London W1T 4LP.

Any person who does any unauthorised act in relation to this publication
may be liable to criminal prosecution and civil claims for damages.

The authors have asserted their right to be identified as the authors of this work
in accordance with the Copyright, Designs and Patents Act 1988.

First published 2006 by
PALGRAVE MACMILLAN
Houndmills, Basingstoke, Hampshire RG21 6XS and
175 Fifth Avenue, New York, N.Y. 10010
Companies and representatives throughout the world

PALGRAVE MACMILLAN is the global academic imprint of the Palgrave
Macmillan division of St. Martin's Press, LLC and of Palgrave Macmillan Ltd.
Macmillan® is a registered trademark in the United States, United Kingdom
and other countries. Palgrave is a registered trademark in the European
Union and other countries.

ISBN13: 978–1–4039–9763–0
ISBN10: 1–4039–9763–2

This book is printed on paper suitable for recycling and made from fully
managed and sustained forest sources.

A catalogue record for this book is available from the British Library.

A catalog record for this book is available from the Library of Congress.

10   9   8   7   6   5   4   3   2   1
15 14 13 12 11 10 09 08 07 06

Printed and bound in Great Britain by
Creative Print & Design (Wales) Ebbw Vale

Many thanks to my lovely parents Ann and Martin, my wonderful husband John, and the best children in the world, Isabel, Caitlin, and Jonjo   (S.R.)

To all our colleagues, past and present, at Cape Consulting, and of course to Chris   (L.E.)

Contents

Contents

Contents

Figures and tables

Figures

Table

Preface

Customers are placing increasing emphasis on the way they are treated. If you want to keep your customers, you have to make sure they feel impressed, not just "OK." You have to earn their confidence and trust—not just once but again and again. You have to make your customers feel important and appreciated, and you have to devise a way to break through all the marketing clutter . . . and all the filters your worldly-wise and increasingly cynical customers have invented to deal with this clutter.

We're going to tell you how to do this.

The good news is that your customers, being human, make largely *emotional* decisions. While you must create compelling, differentiating value for them, keeping them happy doesn't have to mean throwing money, discounts, or free alarm clocks at them. It can be as simple as a follow-up question, a frank acknowledgment to them that you value their continued business, or a sincere smile from a relaxed and motivated employee who genuinely loves serving them. It can happen face-to-face or over the phone, provided you have created the conditions that make it both possible—and probable.

We've written this book, *Customer Loyalty: a guide for time travelers*, because we believe it is high time a new perspective was developed on the matter of winning customer loyalty.

A service business sells itself and when it does this successfully, it makes friends with its customers. The feelings it should generate in its customers are something akin to what a good friendship delivers—feeling important and individual, a sense of being listened to, knowing whom you can trust and who will have the time for a useful chat. Not surprisingly, successful service brands—like the bank First Direct and the UK travel and insurance giant Saga—take the concept one step even further, creating in their customer base a sense of belonging to an exclusive club. This is why today, about one in eight people in the United Kingdom aged 50 or older are Saga customers and First Direct is the United Kingdom's most recommended bank.

Preface

In the course of our research with the customers of a great many service brands, we have discovered a forgotten secret. It's this:

If we have found a service brand that we can make friends with, why on earth would we want to shop around?

It seems organizations have forgotten that customers *prefer* to be loyal.

So what evidence do we have for this assertion? The best evidence of all—the evidence of hindsight. Ever since commercial enterprise began on any large and organized scale, there has been clear evidence that people like brands. They particularly like feeling good about the choices they make, since these choices confer emotional benefits. In the past—just as in the present—product brands conveyed the reassurance of quality, prestige, discernment. Today service brands are doing the same and more—the choice of a service brand has the capacity to convey the emotional benefit of making life easier and more pleasurable. There is little doubt that the importance of service brands is continuing to increase.

Here, in this book, we argue that customers don't want to be shopping around for service brands if they can avoid it. Our lives in the twenty-first century are influenced by a number of significant social trends that actually preclude against too much shopping around, even if we wanted to do it, which we don't. *We haven't got the time for it and we don't know who we can really trust.* Too much choice gives us additional stress. We want to be treated with respect as an individual and not as a member of a target "demographic."

For organizations to create the right type of feelings in customers is no small challenge, but the potential benefits are enormous. It can create the opportunity for some premium in a competitive world—a loyal customer base can boost the bottom line dramatically. It's definitely worth the effort.

In the course of this book we'll be sharing with you real-world examples of some of the actions that service businesses have taken to impress their customers and win their loyalty. Some of these businesses are our clients, some of them are businesses that have impressed us as customers, and some of them fall into both categories. Here is a brief introduction to each of the organizations that feature in the book.

- *Bank of China*. Established in 1912, Bank of China is China's oldest bank. It is also the only Chinese bank with a presence in all the major continents, with over 560 overseas offices in 25 countries and regions. *The Banker* magazine ranks it as one of the world's top banks in terms of core capital. Since its foundation over 90 years ago, Bank of China has played a major role in promoting China's economic and social progress through its active involvement in the country's international trade and financial activities. Since 1992 *Euromoney* magazine has awarded the Bank "The Best Bank in China" nine times. The Bank has also been included in the Fortune Global 500 for 13 consecutive years.
- *Bank of Ireland*. Bank of Ireland first opened its doors to the public over 220 years ago when it received its Royal Charter in Dublin in 1783. Today the bank has over 17 000 employees in eight countries worldwide. It is the largest Irish bank by total assets.
- *Egnatia Bank*. Greece's relatively new Egnatia Bank was founded in 1991, and quickly emerged as one of Greece's fastest growing and most innovative banks. It was the first Greek bank to offer Internet banking services in 1997, and in 1998 was the first Greek bank to offer secure credit card transactions over the Internet. In 2002, Egnatia saw an opportunity to significantly improve customer service, control costs, and boost revenue potential by introducing a modern, multichannel telebanking customer relationship management (CRM) solution. The new system enabled Egnatia to expand the types of services available through its call centers, add interactive voice response (IVR) options, extend service hours to 24/7, and increase the efficiency of phone interactions so customers spent less time on hold.
- *First Direct*. First Direct is the UK's most recommended bank—one in every three customers has been recommended by a current customer. First Direct was formed in 1989 by Midland Bank, now part of HSBC. In the 1980s Midland Bank had the foresight to see that a new bank offering a "direct proposition" for customers could be a major success. Midland Bank commissioned research that revealed customers were making fewer visits to their bank branch and having less contact with staff. The research found this was especially true of certain customer types, such as busy, urban, demanding, professional, educated consumers. Today, First Direct

Preface

employs about 3000 people. It experiences significantly lower than average employee turnover for the sector. It operates its 24-hour online services from two UK contact centers.

- *Holmes Place*. The first Holmes Place health club opened in an old plumbers' merchant's off the Fulham Road in Chelsea, London in 1980. It quickly grew into a chain of clubs, funded in part by outside investors and joint ventures with property development companies. By 1995 the company was awarded its first council leisure contract and it became the first company to have its council leisure contract renewed. The company floated on the London Stock Exchange in November 1997 and has continued to grow steadily. Today, there are 61 Holmes Place clubs—46 in the United Kingdom, 14 in Continental Europe as well as one joint venture club in Chicago.

- *Laithwaites*. Laithwaites is the world's largest mail order wine company. It was formed by Tony and Barbara Laithwaite in 1969, after Tony Laithwaite had a letter published in *The Sunday Times* responding to an article lamenting the poor quality and availability of wine in the United Kingdom. He got 2000 letters agreeing with him. Tony Laithwaite contacted the paper's editor and *The Sunday Times* Wine Club was born. The company grew between 1994–2004 from £42 million turnover to £250 million. It has 800 employees and very low staff turnover. Its main customer contact resources consist of two contact centers with a total of 500 seats. Many managers started at the bottom of the company and have worked their way up. Laithwaites was the winner of the UK's prestigious National Sales Awards 2005.

- *Norwich Union*. With 13 000 employees and total annual premiums of almost £8 billion, Norwich Union Insurance, the general insurance arm of Aviva plc, is the UK's largest insurer. Norwich Union provides 60 percent of Aviva's worldwide general insurance business by gross written premium. In 2004 Norwich Union generated an operating profit of £832 million. Altogether it operates 15 customer contact centers in the United Kingdom and 3 in India. These employ a total of 8000 people.

Our sincere gratitude to those who kindly gave their time, despite having busy schedules, in order that we could research the excellent work their organizations have done in the area of winning customer loyalty. In particular we thank: Lesley Cotton (Holmes Place),

Christos Filinis (Egnatia Bank), Matthew Higgins (First Direct), Brian Lande (Bank of Ireland), F. C. Li (Bank of China), Victoria Sherston (Laithwaites Wines), Stella Stavropoulu (Egnatia Bank), and John Willmott (Norwich Union Insurance).

We also wish to extend our thanks to our colleagues at Cape Consulting for their help and encouragement with this book. Our gratitude to Yannis Anastasiadis, Coral Atkins, Louise Clark, Jamie Craig, Tracey Nunn, Jackie Walpole, Hadrian Wise, and Alex Zitrides. Particular thanks to Brenda Stewart for her significant input to Chapter 4. Our thanks also to our public relations and writing consultant, James Essinger.

Finally, why a guide for time travelers? Because our case is indeed that organizations wishing to succeed in the current demanding environment need to be something like time travelers, and should attune themselves to the ongoing changes in society that matter as far as winning customer loyalty is concerned. Oh, and they especially need to learn the strategic and tactical lessons of the past, too, because that is the best way to understand the present. And, for that matter, the future.

So here it is, *Customer Loyalty: a guide for time travelers*. A guide, in effect, for people for whom developing a skill at winning customer loyalty is an important aspect of their career progression.

A guide, therefore, for everyone in business today.

Dr Sionade Robinson and Lyn Etherington
2005

1   What do customers want?

Winning customers and keeping them coming back are the most hard-fought elements of modern business. Things are fought over because they are precious, and an organization's ability to win customers and to keep customers coming back are indeed extremely precious attributes.

A competitive marketplace requires organizations to find ways to establish relationships with customers that make individual businesses stand out from the crowd. Some commentators might call this process wowing or delighting the customer, while others call it enhancing the customer's experience. We call it *impressing* customers because impressed customers talk about your company. They offer positive opinions, both prompted and unprompted. They share what they have experienced and they stake their personal reputations on the firm belief that others, too, could benefit from doing business with the company they have chosen. When that happens, a business grows.

This book is all about how to grow the number of impressed customers that will want to talk about your business. If you put our advice into practice, your customers will want to tell others about the great service experiences they've had at your company. We can show you how to do this because we know what customers are looking for from service relationships—we know how customers want to feel.

The customer's desire to be loyal

Over the last ten years we have been advising service businesses on improving the quality of relationships they form with their customers in order that our clients can achieve profitable growth. And here's the scoop. When customers feel they are dealing with the right company or organization for their needs, they don't want to change. In fact, they *want* to be loyal.

Why do we believe this to be true in the face of many commentators arguing the opposite? *It's because customers tell us that staying with a supplier that meets their needs and cares about them makes their lives easier.* It's a bit like forming a friendship. We are drawn to people who meet certain criteria—be it their warmth, kindness, dependability, or even their energy and wit—and then we stick with them. We don't make a choice every day about whether to maintain a friendship or not—we just do.

When customers don't want to be loyal, it is normally for one of three reasons. First, the customer may believe that there is always a better deal or better service around the corner. This characteristic may be a function of a customer's personality—they may be "maximizing," constantly driven to find the best—be it an insurance plan, banking service, or even a car mechanic. With the plethora of inescapable marketing messages bombarding customers every day, it's hard not to adopt maximizing tendencies.

Second, customers may not be loyal to an organization because actually that business *can't* meet their needs. If the customer actually likes and wants face to face, personal service, then choosing the lowest cost provider who is running a busy contact center will prove a disappointment.

Third, customers leave suppliers because something has gone wrong in the relationship. The American Management Association recently published an analysis of customer defections in the United States, and found that 13 percent of defections were due to product performance, 12 percent were due to "other reasons" and a massive 75 percent due to shortcomings in customer service. Customers today don't leave because they are dissatisfied, but more because they are not overwhelmingly satisfied and have other choices. This is the point. Failing to meet the customer's expectations and desire for service is enough to prompt a defection. If there were fewer disappointing service experiences there would be fewer defections. It really is as simple as that.

Why merely satisfying customers isn't enough

Once upon a time most business books about customer service tended to focus principally on presenting strategies to deliver satisfied customers. Then in 1995, Thomas O. Jones and W. Earl Sasser Jr showed in "Why satisfied customers defect" (1995) that *satisfying customers is not enough to retain them.*

Why? Because, if one looks at how business really works, even

2

customers claiming to be satisfied defect at a high rate in many industries. There is no simple linear relationship between degrees of satisfaction and the customers' willingness to repurchase. In 1994, Rank Xerox disclosed results of an annual poll of its 480 000 customers. These customers scored their satisfaction with Rank Xerox's products and services using a scale from 1 (low) to 5 (high). Xerox's goal was to achieve 100 percent of responses in the 4 (satisfied) or 5 (very satisfied) band. However its analysis of the relationship between satisfaction scores and customer loyalty revealed that that even among this band, customers scoring their satisfaction as 5 (very satisfied) were six times more likely to re-purchase during the following 18 months than those awarding a 4 (satisfied). This result led Xerox to revise its goals to achievement of 100 percent scoring of 5—very satisfied.

As a result of the Xerox findings back in the 1990s, the compelling view was that businesses must seek 100 percent, or total, customer satisfaction to achieve the kind of predictable repurchase behavior from customers they desired. Nowadays customer satisfaction is almost taken for granted even though satisfaction itself is a relatively low standard. Many of the organizations we have met have reported high satisfaction scores even approaching the 100 percent maximum—but no loyalty. That customers now expect to be highly satisfied is the norm, and any business wishing to secure a stronger bond with their customers must do a great deal more than satisfy. Instead, they must secure an emotional or attitudinal preference or attachment via the customers' feelings.

After the cracks started to show in strategies based on satisfying customers, several studies emerged focusing on the opposite end of the satisfaction continuum—that is, the factors which caused dissatisfaction. For example, Bell and Zemke in their 1987 article, "Service breakdown: the road to recovery," suggested that customers who have experienced service failures fall into two categories—the "annoyed" and the "victimized." Bell and Zemke define annoyance as "minor irritation" associated with a promise not fully realized; whereas a feeling of "victimization" is characterized by a major feeling of "ire, frustration, and/or pain." The interest in sources and degrees of dissatisfaction spawned the industries of service recovery and again studies revealed some strategies for recovering customers were so effective that some customers became more strongly attached to the organization than if nothing had upset them in the first place.

Interestingly, in the analysis of dissatisfaction, it was the customers' feelings—both rational and irrational—that came to the fore, whereas in many satisfaction studies it was the stimulus and response approach that received greater emphasis. Clearly, the feeling of being "victimized" is a deeper and more volatile emotion than feeling mildly irritated and a much more useful term than "dissatisfaction" when communicating with front-line staff about the importance of avoiding this customer reaction. It is the sense of being outraged victims that causes customers to tell stories about their unhappy service experiences far and wide, often with increasing degrees of embellishment and often for many, many years. Think of when you last heard such a story. It's usual for people to join in this type of tale with relish, each competing to top the justifiable sense of outrage that's been provoked by some careless member of staff or unfriendly process. It has been estimated that customers will remember and repeat bad service stories for something like 13 years! A customer who feels victimized bears a serious grudge.

These days, in our research, we have found most customers can comfortably score their overall experience of service businesses in the range "good to very good." Yet despite this, *many customers are essentially ambivalent in their loyalty to a particular business.* These are the customers who would be likely to "defect" in the presence of even a modest motivator—for example, getting a better price, or being intrigued by a new marketing message from another supplier. An "impressed" customer however, feels far less ambivalent. While a "victimized" customer is almost certain to leave a supplier for another and probably become what Jones and Sasser called a "terrorist," a truly impressed customer is likely to become loyal as a result of an organization's good service deeds. Having experienced an organization's superior service, such a customer has faith and will spread the word through *unsolicited advocacy.*

The need to impress customers

These insights suggest organizations should focus on how to create the feelings which impress customers and make a positive impact on customer behavior and loyalty. Above all, organizations must avoid creating feelings of irritation or in extreme cases, victimization or—as we shall describe—simply *no feelings* at all. If organizations can manage customers' emotional responses to service encounters—they can impress. As we've said, impressed customers lead to loyalty.

We define customer loyalty as:

An emotional and attitude-based preference resulting in the behavior of spontaneous personal recommendation and/or purchase.

Customer *loyalty* must be seen as clearly distinct from customer *satisfaction*, which is a predominantly rational and less emotional frame of mind. Loyalty is different from repurchase intent because repurchase may be based merely on inertia. The key factor is the element of *personal recommendation*. In other words, the willingness to stake one's reputation on the future performance of an organization is really the distinguishing feature of the truly loyal customer.

Understanding what customers want

Here, we look at the importance of understanding what customers want from service encounters and how companies can create the feelings in customers that allow service encounters to impress. These two factors—first, understanding what customers want, and second, knowing how to create the feelings that impress customers—underpin our approach to developing the kind of relationships between customers and their chosen providers that can be described as loyal.

The Saga story

If Sidney de Haan, the founder of the Saga Group, had only ever managed merely to satisfy his customers, he would never have grown his business activities beyond running a successful hotel in the seaside resort of Folkestone in the south of England.

Sidney had started out as a hotelier in the late 1940s but had found that while it was easy to fill his hotel in the summer, business was too quiet in the winter. So utilizing the kind of creative insight—propelled by the need to win commercial success—that distinguishes a true entrepreneur from a run-of-the-mill businessperson, he traveled to the north of England, to unglamorous towns that were mainly far from the sea, and offered old age pensioners cheap winter holidays in Folkestone. He found an abundance of customers in the north of England, and soon his hotel was full all year round. He went on to buy other hotels and by following the same business principle he managed to fill those too.

Presently it dawned on Sidney that he could offer his old age pensioners (these were the days before more tactful descriptions such as "senior citizens" became popular) other types of holiday. Before long he had set up a business he called "The Old People's Travel Bureau."

Not a very glamorous name, perhaps, but an unambiguous one which conveyed the simplicity, attention to detail, and value for money his not very wealthy customers appreciated. From the outset, Sidney decided he would create a business that would focus on retired people, and that he would sell to his customers directly rather than through intermediaries (such as travel agencies) and constantly strive to offer his customers value for money. The Old People's Travel Bureau prospered. All the same, the brand name did perhaps lack a certain something, so some years later he thought of a better name that rather brilliantly encapsulated all the positive aspects of longevity: Saga.

Saga is today a major brand in the area of financial services and travel, with about one-eighth of the UK population over the age of 50 forming its customer base. In 2005 the de Haan family sold the Saga Group for £1.4 billion. Saga is run under new management that adheres meticulously to Sidney's guiding principles of:

- focusing on providing older customers with products and services that are tailored to their needs (though the Saga age threshold is now just 50)
- selling to customers directly rather than through agencies and intermediaries
- understanding how to impress customers and thereby increase their perception of value for money.

In setting up and running Saga, it is evident that Sidney de Haan had spotted a unique opportunity to meet the needs of this specific customer group. And there is an interesting and important lesson here. His success was based on understanding people's needs— spoken and unspoken—rather than the more conventional model that focuses on customer expectations. He impressed his customers—as Saga still does—creating in them the kinds of feelings that make many customers see Saga as a special club rather than a commercial business.

Understanding customer behavior

Many of the models used for the analysis of customer research are based almost exclusively on presenting a detailed overview of customer expectations (such as Zeithaml, Parasuraman, and Berry's *Balancing Customer Perceptions and Expectations,* 1990). This is based on the premise that it is the gap between customers' expectations and the reality of their experience that form the basis of subsequent evaluation, leading to:

- satisfaction (where there is no gap and expectations match experience)
- dissatisfaction (where the expectations exceed experience)
- the opportunity to delight customers (where experience exceeds expectations).

Approaches that focus on developing in-depth understanding of customers' expectations have, of course, proved extremely useful to organizations. They are predominantly qualitative and can provide companies with:

- customers' overall service expectations
- customers' detailed expectations with regard to specific service scenarios
- the relative priorities of different elements of service
- qualitative perceptions of a company's current performance.

In such groups, customers are selected by various criteria to populate a relatively homogenous discussion group. A skilled facilitator might ask customers to describe their view of ideal service (or *expected* service, or *best in class* service), and then discuss this with reference to a particular organization's performance. They may be asked to rank or "trade off" various service attributes. Client organizations receive a list of service attributes along with desired service standards. They also receive customer views on their own perceived performance against the ideal—sometimes comparing that performance against other competitive organizations with whom the customer has experience. The list of service attributes are usually ranked in terms of importance—the idea being that different customer groups may value attributes of service differently.

While we acknowledge that this body of research is well founded, we also argue that it does not focus sufficiently on what we know about customers' emotional needs. By far the most famous index of human desires is psychologist Abraham Maslow's hierarchy of needs. Maslow, the founder of the humanist school of psychology, described a hierarchy ranging from the bottom, the physiological needs for simple bodily survival to the uppermost need—to self actualize or fulfill one's potential. Maslow argued that one could hardly self actualize through the appreciation of beauty if, for example, every moment was a desperate struggle for food, warmth, or safety.

Fortunately in the developed world, few of us are required to struggle to meet physiological needs. But what of our other needs? We argue that it is the organizations which meet customers' emotional needs that create feelings of being impressed. Organizations which do this stand out from the competitive crowd. We argue strongly that it is whether and how the customers' psychological needs are met—the need for esteem, for instance—that result in positive or negative feelings about an organization.

For example, consider the case of the online supermarket that fails to deliver ordered groceries on the allotted day. This could be framed

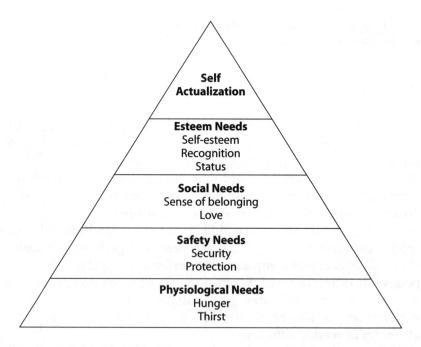

Figure 1 Maslow's hierarchy of needs

as an instance of unfulfilled expectations—yet the resultant anger and rage ignited in the customer seem incongruously out of proportion with mere unmet expectations. However by rethinking the situation as one that violated the customer's fundamental need to be treated with respect, we can more readily accept and anticipate the customer's feelings of anger and outrage.

First then, we will briefly review the conventional model of customer satisfaction and follow that with a fuller treatment of a complementary needs-based model.

Modeling customer expectations

Typically, conventional models of customer satisfaction are implicitly or explicitly variations of the "met-expectations model" (also known as the "gap model" or "disconfirmation of expectations").

This framework assumes that customers have specific expectations about their interactions with an organization and, by meeting those expectations, the organization can satisfy the customer. Customer satisfaction models are often quite complex. For example, some models differentiate between perceptions of quality and customer satisfaction (quality being only one component of satisfaction), and others use various approaches to assess "expectations" (what should *be*, what is *ideal*, or what is *realistically expected*). All focus on satisfying the customer's expectations of the attributes being delivered—whether those attributes relate to facets of service quality, or perceived value.

It's true that expectations models do overlap somewhat into the area of what it takes to delight a customer—one element in our concept of the need to impress. Expectations research generally shows that exceeding customer expectations causes customer delight. Whereas perceived quality and satisfaction result from *meeting* customer expectations, delight may result from providing the customer with more than expected. Pleasant surprises, so to speak, create delighted customers. But how could a service business act to continually provide the pleasant surprises that increase customer delight?

First, the firm would need to research its customers' expectations—this time their experience-based expectations, rather than ideal or normative expectations. To elicit a pleasant surprise requires an organization to know what its customers expect (experience-based expectations) or their predictions about the outcome of their next exchange with the organization. Delight is delivered when the firm provides a surprising, positive departure from expectations. For example, if a dry cleaning customer is treated to free service in reward for loyal patronage, delight results primarily because the customer had predicted (expected) the need to pay.

Difficulties occur though, in the pragmatic application of such an insight. In our experience, several organizations have sought research to show how to consistently "delight" or "wow" their customers. One famous hotel chain badgered us to provide examples of ideas which would deliver repeated customer "delight"—as if the "pleasant surprises" which engender delight could thereafter be mass-produced, to thereby create a loyal customer base, irrespective of customers' individual needs.

In summary, achieving delight and engendering the loyalty that ostensibly follows in the expectations model can be elusive for two reasons. First, there is the obvious assertion that most customers do not feel especially "delighted" or become loyal when an organization is merely delivering the basics of the service promise (see the RATER definitions in Table 1).

Research shows that after fulfilling basic reliability expectations, an organization then must meet expectations related to responsiveness and assurance to enhance loyalty. Thereafter, it must meet expectations for empathy to receive yet another boost. Fulfilling expectations to promote loyalty is a dynamic rather than static construct—expectation levels are always ratcheting upward. Expectations are dynamic—as are customers' feelings.

Reliability	The ability to provide what was promised, dependably and accurately
Assurance	The knowledge and courtesy of employees; their ability to convey trust and confidence
Tangibles	The physical functionality of service facilities including their appearance
Empathy	The degree of caring and individual attention
Responsiveness	The willingness to help and provide prompt service; problem solving

Table 1 The RATER framework

Second, customers are individuals and what constitutes pleasant surprises in excess of expected levels of service will vary. This makes them difficult to measure for research purposes and also difficult to manage. Generally speaking, seeking to systematically evoke customer delight by exceeding expectations is an extremely difficult and very expensive way to build loyal customers.

The primacy of customers' feelings

Though useful for understanding at a rational level customers' satisfaction and dissatisfaction, we believe that the expectations model is less helpful in offering insights into customers' emotions. *Much more important is understanding how to positively impact customers' feelings and to keep them coming back and talking about the great company with whom they are dealing.*

At this stage we also need to differentiate between the concepts of customer delight and a broader concept of impressing customers. We have already defined customer delight as the "pleasant surprise" when service positively deviates from expectations.

Impressing customers, however, is more about understanding how to consistently create the feelings that inspire customers to feel themselves to be individually valued and important. These are customer reactions that are more emotionally charged than mere satisfaction or dissatisfaction. We believe organizations cannot elicit the desired emotionally charged responses from customers necessary to impress them (or avoid being victims) by focusing only on meeting or exceeding specific service expectations. We need another perspective.

Instead, to explain how to impress customers, we'll review why certain customer feelings can cause them to be impressed with an organization. We have identified these feelings in the course of ten years of consulting work and research with service businesses. When front-line service providers understand the significance of their own behavior in creating these feelings, customers exit service encounters feeling *impressed* with the experience. We call these customer feelings Loyalty-building experiences (LBEs). When they are consistently perceived to be of a high standard, our research shows that they create loyal customers.

LBEs can be defined as "recognizable and measurable feelings that impress and create a willingness to recommend to others." We enlarge in detail upon the nature of LBEs later in this book.

The new age of customer loyalty

In today's buying world, where customers are confronted by a vast number of offerings streaming towards them from numerous sources, both physical and virtual, organizations may be forgiven for assuming that the age of customer loyalty is over. They may easily conclude that everything is being brought down to the level of a commodity—with the implication that price is the only factor that matters.

Price certainly *is* important when customers make spending choices. But in practice sheer common sense, and the fact that markets have plenty of room for players who are *not* the lowest-cost provider, tells us that other factors really matter too. Just as we make allowances for friends, so do loyal customers, within reasonable limits, tolerate a price differential—a small premium in recognition of a valuable relationship.

In particular, customers badly want to feel good about the level of service they receive from an organization, and want to feel that the organization genuinely cares about them and their needs. But what can we say about the nature of these needs and how meeting them can positively impact loyalty?

Schneider and Bowen in their book, *Winning the Service Game* (1995) argue that for a service business, customers' emotional responses originate in three basic customer *needs*—those of security, justice, and self-esteem—and how they are handled.

Schneider and Bowen begin with two basic premises, namely:

- Customers are people first and consumers second.
- People strive to satisfy core needs in life at a level more funda-mental and compelling than meeting their specific expectations as consumers.

By thinking of customers as consumers, an organization focuses on service performance attributes and how to meet or exceed consumer expectations. *Thinking of customers foremost as people shifts the emphasis to basic human needs.* The impulse on the part of people to fulfill these basic needs is sacrosanct; violate these needs and the outcome will be outrage and victimization; fulfill them and the result will be to impress.

How needs shape customer behavior

Expectations and needs shape customer behavior. The desired outcome of expectations is getting what one anticipates from a service encounter as a consumer; needs focus on obtaining what one seeks from life as a person. Expectations can be satisfied; needs are such that they must be continually and consistently attended to—by every customer contact point in an organization.

Three needs: an overview

The hierarchy of customer needs identified in 1943 by Abraham Maslow in his article "A theory of human motivation" has a relatively long history of application in management. In explaining how to impress customers and create LBEs we have borrowed specifically two of Maslow's needs—the needs for security and self-esteem—and a third from Schneider and Bowen—the need to be treated fairly, which underpins the notion of having "trust" in a company.

Specifically, "security" refers to the need to feel unthreatened by economic or indeed physical harm. "Self-esteem" refers to the need to maintain and enhance one's self-image and the need to be treated fairly requires no further explanation. These three needs help to explain why LBEs are so effective.

At Cape Consulting, our own experience in consulting to, and research with, service businesses suggests that the best way to "manage" customers' needs for security and to be treated fairly is to avoid violating them through service failures in the first place.

Violation of these needs will usually incite a sense of outrage; however, respecting these two needs is more likely to produce a passive sense of satisfaction rather than overtly impressing the customer. In contrast, where a customer's esteem is bolstered—and he or she is left feeling smarter, listened to, respected, and valued—the customer is much more likely to be impressed with the service encounter.

Security

Most customers do not know when their security needs have been met because they are generally unaware of them in the first place, unless there has been a problem of some sort. The key factor in meeting security needs is whether customers believe they can entrust their well-being to another. Customers with a low risk preference for investments must feel that an advisor has taken this into consideration if they, the customers, are to feel secure. Witness the furore over the mis-selling scandals in the United Kingdom in the pensions market, or the collapse of the long-trusted financial institution Equitable Life. The justifiable outrage unleashed when those companies failed to meet customers' need to feel unthreatened by economic harm rumbles on and on.

With regard to the need for security, let's consider whether positive deviations from stability, routine, and equilibrium might yield positive consequences. It's our belief that people seek consistency, equilibrium, and stability in their lives; in other words, customers would prefer to be loyal. But what if leaving this stable state created a benefit for the customer—a cheaper mortgage rate, for example, than that being offered by the current provider? Such a positive outcome would obviously delight the customer in that he or she had found a better rate. At the same time, finding a better rate with a competitor would totally undermine a customer's sense of, and need for, security. It's for this reason that most customers switch without offering their incumbent provider the opportunity to match any marketplace deal.

Perceived fairness

Maslow's theory does not explicitly discuss the need for fairness, though considerable research in philosophy and social psychology suggests that the notion of fairness is absolutely central to relationships within society and between individuals. Interestingly, Leonard Berry has noted in his 1995 book *On Great Service*:

> *The service promise ... includes the implicit promise of fair play. Customers expect service companies to treat them fairly; they become angry and mistrustful when they perceive otherwise.*

Needs related to perceived fairness are not as crucial for survival as security needs; violation of the need for fairness does not threaten life nor financial security. Nevertheless, the need for fairness, and its consequent outcome, trust, does become important when considering relationships with customers as a two-way street.

We commonly recognize the investment an organization makes in attracting customers, acquiring customers, and in delivering a specific service, but seldom do we think of the emotional investment a customer makes in an organization. At Cape Consulting we have often held focus groups for our insurance clients where customers describe

14

the following two frustrations, both based on *perceived* unfairness of the insurance system.

> *I invest time, money, and effort in patronizing this business and continually demonstrate loyalty to the business by renewing my policy. Yet, after I had one accident, the company raised my rates. I have been loyally paying premiums for many years, and now the company has been charging me higher fees for three years! What about all those years when I paid premiums and never had an accident?*

Alternatively

> *I have been a loyal customer for years and never claimed for a thing. Then when I spilt paint on my carpet, I assumed I would be covered for a replacement. It turned out—in the small print—that I wasn't actually covered for this type of accident. But surely after ten years' loyalty, they would allow me to get a new carpet?*

Respecting the customer's need for fairness means delivering service at three levels. First, Bowen and Schneider refer to ensuring the customer perceives *distributive justice* involving the customer's evaluation of the outcome of the encounter. Second is *procedural justice*, in which customers judge the fairness of rules and procedures, and third, *interactional justice*, which involves how an organization's employees relate, on a personal level, with the customers: their "bedside manner," so to speak.

The first, distributive justice, is difficult to manage because customers use some combination of three often internally inconsistent rules (equity, equality, and needs) to determine if an organization is acting fairly. The equity rule implies that if individuals invest a certain amount of effort, time, or money, an organization should reciprocate proportionately. For example, people who have paid on insurance policies for years without filing a claim may feel they should not experience rate increases the first time they have an accident.

The equality rule implies that everyone is treated the same way: for example, if a policy does not cover spilt paint, then the rules cannot be bent for some customers and not others. The needs rule implies that, on the basis of unique, individual requirements, firms may decide to treat people differently. Inconsistency is clearly in evidence therefore, when a customer define fairness as being treated the same as *some* other customers (on the basis of equity), the same as *all* other customers (on the basis of equality), or like *no other* customer (on the basis of his or her individual circumstances or need).

In the service business, some airlines appear to have got the complex management challenge right. For example, some airlines employ the equity principle by stating clearly that first-class customers get more service than those who invest less. Airlines publicly declare what they will do for the investment their passengers make and then deliver it without economy class passengers feeling unfairly treated. The secret of the airlines' success is that everyone knows the ground rules—what you'll get for a first class investment versus an economy ticket. (Admittedly, the perceived value of such an investment is now clearly in question given the increase in low-cost airlines which make a virtue of offering little or no service beyond transfer from A to B.)

Airlines have also addressed the issues of equality and individual need. Everyone in economy gets the same food (or not) regardless of his or her fare base. Passengers do not board the aircraft wearing their fare base codes for all to see (though again, this is now a popular topic—and a source of esteem—among low-cost travelers!). How about individual need? Some airlines give additional boarding time to parents traveling with children—though some don't. Some also care for disabled passengers or those requiring additional help in transferring to aircraft—though some don't. The key to success, when need is a basis for action, is the publicly known reason for different types of treatment. When differential treatment occurs, as in cases of need or equity, the reason for that treatment must be public, otherwise people will expect equality.

The secret to fulfilling a customer's need for equity justice is literally, or at least figuratively, to compensate the person for investments of time, effort, and money. For example, insurance actuaries could be challenged to differentiate long-term policyholders from short-termers when calculating the probabilities of having a second accident for the potential assessment of premium increases. The ten-year anniversaries of insurance policies could yield a bonus to the policy. A seemingly minor corporate investment in terms of cost, such a gesture could be a psychologically equitable acknowledgment of customer loyalty. By demonstrating loyalty to the customer, an organization hopes for customer loyalty in return.

The importance of procedural fairness and "bedside manner" is evident in our research on what customers really want from service firms:

- *Keeping promises and commitments*: companies need to keep promises, especially when time is the issue; when people have a reservation or a specific time commitment they don't want to wait.
- *Help when needed*: companies are unjust if they don't help someone who needs help.
- *Friendliness*: companies should treat people with openness and warmth.
- *Honesty*: companies shouldn't lie to customers.
- *Politeness*: companies should treat people courteously and respectfully.
- *Flexibility in dealing with unusual requests*: companies should strive to honor reasonable yet out-of-the-ordinary requests. ·

What's interesting about the items listed above is that they largely depend on how an organization treats its own people. These factors can only be provided by highly skilled, motivated, and empowered service providers. In fact the customers' perceived fairness of the outcomes of service encounters and a company's service procedures depends almost totally on processes and procedures that must be skillfully taught, reinforced, delivered, and monitored.

What happens when a business does not behave in a way that customers perceive as fair? The company loses its customers' trust and most probably their loyalty and patronage. Once a company violates trust, how difficult is it to turn back the clock? We would argue that it is close to impossible. We would also argue that the opportunity to impress the customer sufficiently to win their loyalty has been squandered forever. That's not to say that a customer may still return at some time in the future if an offer is good enough, but that customer will never be loyal.

In the meantime it pays to have plans in place to recover from service breakdowns, because errors are inevitable. There will always be disgruntled or angry consumers for whom such plans may be put in motion. Three rules apply to service recovery:

1. *Be quick about it*: fix the problem immediately with no questions asked. If it can't be corrected immediately, follow up with the customer, and keep the customer informed of actions taken and progress made.
2. *Get it right*: an organization gets only one chance to recover. If it fails at service recovery, the outcome will certainly be a customer who feels victimized, a potential customer terrorist and defector.

3. *Leave the customer better off than before*: ensure that the customer feels secure, feels better about himself or herself, and feels justly treated.

The effect of all this effort in meeting customers' needs for perceived fairness is not, however, sufficient to create impressed customers. That is dependent on the characteristics of the next need—that for self-esteem.

Self-esteem

This is the most important need and penultimate in Maslow's hierarchy. Safeguarding and/or building a customer's self-esteem is the key to impressing him or her. It is achieved by enhancing feelings of self-worth, by acknowledging the customer's point of view, sense of importance, and indeed his or her rights. Also, the smarter, more competent, and more valued a customer feels, the more impressed he or she will be at the outcome of the service encounter.

Maintaining and enhancing esteem takes many forms. In preserving a customer's self-esteem, the company may need to foster his or her sense of self-worth, so he or she does not feel or appear stupid. In our work in contact centers, we have frequently heard a customer, when buying holiday insurance for example, share his or her excitement about a pending trip, only to have that emotion ignored by the agent. The outcome is that the customer feels embarrassed and unimportant for daring to share a human emotion with a stranger.

However, the best service organizations—and the best service providers in other organizations—quickly acknowledge the customer's perspective by establishing rapport and soliciting details about a customers need, query, or problem: "It must be great to be going on holiday," "I'd like to understand in detail what's concerning you about this issue," or "I understand that you are upset about this, please tell me exactly what has happened." *Top service businesses treat the customer as an important individual with whom they seek a mutually beneficial relationship, not just as an interchangeable member of a target group.* When service providers at least *appear* to view customers as unique people, customers are impressed.

A second effective way to reaffirm a customer's feeling of confidence and competency is to arrange service environments in ways that permit him or her to feel in control. Customers attending our focus

18

groups over the years have often cited their needs for well-designed signage in service premises, for clarity in queuing systems (reluctantly acknowledging the need for queues), for clear instructions on paperwork, much more frequently than might be anticipated. We believe this is because customers—human beings—wish to avoid appearing confused or ignorant.

No one enjoys feeling stupid, yet service is not synonymous with servility or obsequiousness toward the customer. Overdone efforts to enhance customer self-esteem risk insulting a customer's intelligence. Sharing information in such a way that the customer feels "smarter" as a result reaffirms customer feelings of competency, whereas being condescending or talking down to a customer will never impress and could provoke a much more unpleasant reaction.

Meeting and managing customer needs

Service consists of an exchange relationship: customers exchange their money and loyalty for what we argue is fulfillment of needs—a psychological contract with service firms to have needs met in exchange for money, time, and effort.

In our research over the last ten years we have identified a range of crucially important behaviors which successfully meet customers' needs. The effect of these behaviors is to have an enormously positive impact on customers' feelings and experiences. From among the many emotional responses that a customer may have as a result of an encounter with a service provider, we have isolated eight which describe how customers want to feel. The result of giving customers what they want is evidenced by the loyalty they extend to the organization.

We have called the eight experiences that describe how customers want to feel the loyalty-building experiences (LBEs). When we distilled these important experiences we were tempted to call them loyalty-winning experiences in recognition of their importance. But that would have wrongly implied that each alone was sufficient to impress. More accurately, it is the cumulative effect of the experiences and behaviors that deliver them that creates in the customer the sense of needs met and the desire to recommend.

The LBEs impress because they meet the innate human needs that govern much of our behavior and reaction to the behavior of others. Examples of the behaviors which underpin how LBEs are created include:

- modulating the voice to offer enthusiastic and welcoming greetings and communication
- building rapport by listening for personal information or personal attitudes offered by customers, and using these to develop sincere personal connections such as an "I know just what you mean" kind of interaction
- keeping customers engaged by offering relevant information, appropriate explanations, and insights
- reassuring customers by encouraging them to ask questions and to communicate any further queries they may have.

We describe in depth the origins and the effectiveness of the LBEs later, and also reveal in considerable detail how they can be delivered to customers. But before we descend to that level of detail, consider the earlier arguments about the fundamental nature of the customer exchange relationship—we trade our loyalty as customers for fulfillment of our needs. This means that companies must manage how they implement concern for customer needs in *all* actions that might influence customers' feelings about their relationship with the organization.

This includes the activities of the back office (such as processing and distribution), not just front-office customer contact personnel who interact directly with the customer. To focus on meeting the customers' needs is to concentrate on what it really takes to build relationships. And that will mean questioning an organization's structure from top to bottom.

By contrast, a focus on performing well on service attributes reinforces the fragmented transactional view of service delivery that fails to address the need for a "seamless" customer experience. Building relationships requires that companies view customers as people first and consumers second. Deep understanding of the generic customer needs outlined here, combined with actions to create the type of organization where the LBEs can be consistently delivered, will produce the type of relationship that leads to customer retention and loyalty.

In conclusion, we have outlined the basis of our belief that customers want to be loyal—but only to organizations that can meet their needs. We have outlined why understanding customers' needs and emotions can enable organizations to impress customers. We have also introduced our research which suggests that there are eight key feelings (our LBEs) which will positively impress customers and lead to loyalty for the company that delivers them. In the rest of this book we reveal what an organization must do to make this logical sequence a reality in their business.

But before we do so, it's important to establish whether the investment in strategies to win customer loyalty will stand the test of time—and whether past experience suggests that the investment is likely to be profitable. To ascertain this, we need to become time travelers.

2 Lessons in customer loyalty from the past

We don't usually have too many problems understanding the fundamental motivations of people, and even entire populations, who feature in history. As for art and literature, they retain a power to move us over centuries and even over millennia. These facts, taken together, suggest that human nature does not change much over time, even though the physical environment in which people live and the technology and resources they have do, of course, change a great deal.

This being so, it makes sense to see what lessons we can learn from the past about winning—and losing—customer loyalty. After all, lessons learnt in the past have been paid for by someone else; it seems abundantly sensible to benefit from this free advice if we can.

First steps in exploring customer loyalty in the past

How far back should we begin our investigation of how customer loyalty was won in the past? Recorded history begins in or around the third millennium BC, when the Ancient Sumerians and Ancient Egyptians built the world's first cities. It is no accident that the building of cities coincided with the beginnings of writing itself and the start of recorded history. Hunter-gathering communities can adopt a fairly casual attitude towards personal property, but once people start to settle in towns, property has to be accounted for in a more formal fashion. There is clear archaeological evidence that writing itself first came into being into order to record personal possessions in a reliable way.

Even before the foundation of the world's first cities—such as Babylon in Ancient Mesopotamia—people living in smaller settlements would have competed for customers for whatever they might have to sell, but customer loyalty first started to matter in the early towns and cities, because prior to their foundation, people mainly sold things to people they knew *personally*. Winning customer loyalty is all about winning loyalty from strangers; or at least people who are strangers to start with. Our core idea that customer loyalty is emotionally related to the loyalty we show to friends means that loyal customers do *not* need to continue as strangers for long.

If we look around the world, the bustling, intensely competitive public marketplaces we find in developing countries today are no doubt much the same as they were in the past. Furthermore, these marketplaces in modern developing countries surely give us some idea of what marketplaces were like in the past in developed countries such as the United Kingdom.

We can confidently assume that such marketplaces have always featured intense competition among vendors over price and quality of merchandise, though there is also often covert collusion (generally banned by modern trading legislation) between sellers to stop prices dropping too low.

The bid to win customer loyalty must have been part of business life for many hundreds or thousands of years, even though the vendors at the time may not have seen it this way. *Their* focus was on earning enough to survive another day rather than on winning customer loyalty, but of course ultimately the desire for commercial survival is only another way of expressing the need to win customers and if possible to turn those customers you win into loyal ones. Today, if developed countries did not have welfare provisions, winning customer loyalty would be even more desperate an endeavour than it actually is.

We don't know how "perfect" yesterday's marketplaces were in the economic sense of all customers having access to all information about pricing and goods, but it seems likely that most markets featured several vendors selling approximately the same thing and—initially at least—competing mainly on price.

But some sellers doubtless came to know their customers personally (and so the customers stopped being strangers). Sellers who managed to do this would quickly have attuned themselves to what a particular customer wanted. We don't know for certain, but we can reasonably assume, that sellers who met these personal needs probably succeeded in winning a kind of loyalty from customers even without invariably offering the best price in the marketplace. We know that, today, people like to do business with people and organizations they know. What grounds do we have for thinking that people were any different in the past? As we say, human nature doesn't change.

Customer loyalty in the nineteenth century

There are good reasons for only traveling as far as back in time as the nineteenth century in order to embark on a detailed consideration of the nature of customer loyalty in the past. It is reasonable to assert that before the dawn of the nineteenth century, economies were fairly primitive and featured relatively straightforward buyer/seller relationships which only shed a fairly limited light on the nature of customer loyalty in a modern economy.

But the nineteenth century saw commercial life in the world's most technologically advanced countries (and especially the United Kingdom and the United States) achieve a level of sophistication that was not only unprecedented, but also laid a solid foundation for economic life in the twentieth and twenty-first centuries. It is no accident that the period yielding the first really substantial insights into sellers' responses to customer behavior is indeed the nineteenth century.

The second half of that century is particularly fruitful in terms of the insights it yields. This was a period marked by competition so intense that even today's cut-throat marketplaces seem sedate by comparison. For much of the century there was little or no legislation affecting vendors, and they operated in a sort of laissez-faire free-for-all which however undisciplined it may have been, did at least show human behavior in its rawest and most elemental form.

Furthermore, the very fact that there were no welfare "cushions" to speak of meant that there was inevitably a kind of desperation surrounding individual attempts to succeed. However unpleasant this may have been for the participants, it certainly sharpened their commercial sensibilities. In the nineteenth century, giving customers satisfaction and winning their loyalty was a kind of religion. In the twenty-first century, on the other hand, while you may face relative poverty and social embarrassment if your business fails, you are unlikely to starve. Yet even today we work hard. It is hardly surprising that nineteenth-century people often seem to us to have worked like slaves possessed of a demonic work ethic. They had no other choice.

When we look at nineteenth-century entrepreneurs, we see a tremendous resourcefulness and enterprise as a result of the dire economic penalties that waited on failure. The sheer drive and energy with which so many traders and early businesses sought—often successfully—to win customer loyalty is immensely impressive.

The realities of nineteenth-century life

Despite the romanticized view of life offered by some Victorian novelists—or at least their twentieth-century adapters for the screen—life for most people during the nineteenth-century was hard and impoverished.

Their material possessions, the clothes they wore, and the food and drink they consumed, reflected this. But by around the middle of the nineteenth century, life in some countries—especially the United Kingdom, the United States, and some continental European countries—there was gradually starting to develop a sophisticated and even luxurious aspect for a broader range of people than just those at the very top of society.

In the United Kingdom especially, the Industrial Revolution—which began around 1780 and had its principal impetus from then until about 1850—gradually led to the evolution of a prosperous middle class. These people, unencumbered with anything more than a minimal income tax, were starting to enjoy a standard of living that would have been unthinkable even a couple of generations previously. The middle class could enjoy the pleasures of life in every sense. Nineteenth-century prosperity in effect created a relatively unregulated economic microcosm from which, as business historians looking back in time, we can gain useful insights into winning customer loyalty.

It is no accident that many efforts to win customer loyalty in this period tended to focus on food and drink products. Regulations controlling the production of food and drink to ensure public safety hardly existed. There was ample opportunity for charlatans and unscrupulous business people to deliver a lamentably poor standard of product. Customer choice was especially highly active in food and drink because for many people who were only just emerging from poverty, the first products on which they could exercise a varied choice tended to be food and drink brands. Furthermore, with standards initially being so low, there was indeed abundant opportunity for resourceful manufacturers to design and market products which could win a level of loyalty which brought vast profits. Many of the great nineteenth-century fortunes were won from food and drink brands.

It is important to mention at this stage a distinction that we elaborate on later in Chapter 5. This distinction is between the *product brand*—which is a tangible *thing* that is being sold under a particular branding—and a *service brand*—usually an intangible set of services. The acid test for the distinction between a product brand and service brand is that with a product brand, the organization selling the product brand is not usually of any importance in the promotion of the branding, and in fact many customers will not even know the name of the organization. With a service brand, on the other hand, it is usually the organization itself that is really being promoted rather than the product.

The nineteenth century was the great era of the dawn of *product* brands, just as our early twenty-first century is the great era of *service* brands.

The nineteenth century was, in short, the epoch of people buying *things*. After all, the Industrial Revolution was producing not *services* but tangible *objects*, and this object-focused attitude of the time extended to the culture and to the economy. Look at how the interiors of nineteenth-century houses were cluttered with *things*; the job of dusting them must have been fearsome. While it is true that many product brands first devised in the nineteenth century are still with us today, there are far more other brands which, while popular in the nineteenth century, are forgotten today.

The nineteenth century had a product-oriented commercial culture. Yes, service mattered, very much indeed, but service had not yet, with a very few exceptions, become enshrined in the *brand*. For nineteenth-century customers, a brand meant a *product brand*. That was their world; that was their culture. And to understand their world, and harvest the insights it furnishes that are still useful today, we need to be time travelers.

The Book of Household Management

There is no better indicator of the growing discrimination of consumers of food and drink or the new prosperity of the middle classes than the justly famous work by (Mrs) Isabella Beeton, *The Book of Household Management*, first published in 1861, and still found invaluable by many cooks today.

The book runs to more than 1200 pages, of which about 1000 are concerned with recipes and ideal bills of fare for middle-class households. Meat, fish, and game are very much favored over salads and vegetables. Modern nutritionists might frown upon some of the recipes, which are often alarmingly heavy on eggs and butter, and also are prone to include creatures (blackbirds, for example) which most people nowadays prefer to feed rather than feed on.

Yet Mrs Beeton's acute awareness of the difference between good quality and poor quality food shines through on every page of her book. She was especially concerned that her readers should have the opportunity to enjoy the former rather than the latter.

Indeed, as Mrs Beeton herself explains, her motivation in writing the book was to help women keep their husbands at home by offering them excellent housekeeping in general, and excellent food and drink in particular, rather than lose them to gentlemen's clubs. As Mrs Beeton writes in the Preface to the first edition:

> *What moved me, in the first instance, to attempt a work like this, was the discomfort and suffering which I had seen brought upon men and women, by household mismanagement. I had always thought that there is no more fruitful source of family discontent than a housewife's badly cooked dinners and untidy ways. Men are now so well served out of doors—at their clubs, well-ordered taverns, and dining houses, that, in order to compete with the attractions of these places, a mistress must be thoroughly acquainted with the theory and practice of cookery, as well as be perfectly conversant with all the other arts of making and keeping a comfortable home.*

She goes on to explain that she wrote her book to help wives win domestic loyalty from their husbands.

The advertisements in the back and front of her book are designed to win from readers a more directly commercial kind of loyalty. This kind of loyalty, of course, is what our own book, *Customer Loyalty: a guide for time travelers* is all about. These advertisements clearly demonstrate the desire of early businesses to attract customers to their own products—their own *branded* products. And this meant *product brands*, not service brands.

We have already seen that brands are vital to making your business succeed, and that they are much more than merely an interesting marketing exercise. The nineteenth-century use of brands exemplifies their importance in attracting customer loyalty, and thereby revenue, to one supplier rather than another. Branding in the nineteenth century was a big part of the desperate competitive struggle of the day.

It was the age of the individual, and of individual struggle, in every sense. In his novel *The Man of Property* published in 1906 and later to become the first volume of *The Forsyte Saga* (1922), John Galsworthy writes of the "terrible call to individuality" of London in the nineteenth century. To the modern reader this phrase may conjure up nothing more horrifying than exuberant hairstyles, but in the economic context of the nineteenth century, when failure to win customers' loyalty to your own individual offering meant disaster, it takes on a more somber meaning. In our sophisticated modern economy, where top managers flit from one organization to another at a moment's notice, it's easy to see business as a kind of elaborate game. But it isn't, and it certainly wasn't for the Victorians.

The route to market for most vendors was through their own retail outlet or through a retail outlet to which they sold on a wholesale basis. Difficulties in distribution meant that many products were sold near their production site, even when they were sold wholesale. Factories could operate close to the center of cities at a time when property prices were not what they are now.

For businesses operating in these conditions, there must have been, as well as a dread of failure, a glorious sense—even an intoxicatingly glorious sense—of opportunity. Distinguishing oneself from the crowd—that process of differentiation which is as important today as it ever was—lay at the heart of all nineteenth-century enterprise. And if one failed to achieve this differentiation? The penalty would be commercial failure, and possible destitution. At first these differentiations took the form of simple *brandings,* with just the vendor's or manufacturer's name followed by the generic name of the product, for example, Smith's Black Puddings. Many of these products were food-related, but as the century wore on, brandings were extended to a wider range of products.

Looking at an 1880 edition of Mrs Beeton's book, we see advertisements for brand-name medicines, pocket-handkerchiefs, marking ink, and even ice machines. These ice machines are advertised so proudly, one easily forgets they were not refrigerators in the modern sense of the word, but simply ice-cupboards that would keep lake ice (a popular consumer product in Victorian London) in its solid, wintry state for as long as possible.

One particularly entrepreneurial vendor, George Nelson of 14 Dowgate Hill, London, offers readers Nelson's gelatine, Nelson's citric acid, and Nelson's essence of lemon, all of which were used in the making of jellies—considered at the time to be a particularly nutritious foodstuff. If jellies were not to your taste, you could purchase Nelson's pure beef tea, which probably tasted something like modern-day Bovril, and was available in half-pint packets.

Notice how the branding in this instance is a simple matter of attaching the surname of the manufacturer to the generic name of the product. George Nelson knew he had to demonstrate the quality of his particular branded products. He signs his advertisements personally and emphasizes that he has been awarded a Royal Warrant because his products are used by royalty. He is evidently particularly proud of his beef tea, which he describes as a "readily digestible food for invalids." George Nelson lists a testimonial from the medical magazine *The Lancet*. which recommends Nelson's beef tea as:

An excellent preparation. Is very portable. Its flavour is all that could be desired.

The *Medical Press* is quoted as saying:

One of the best articles of the class we have examined.

The firm also offers Nelson's soups, which are described in more restrained terms as being:

Beef, with various kinds of vegetables, carrots, celery etc.

By 1880, advertisements for food brands such as this were ubiquitous in the newspapers and household journals likely to be read by the middle classes and aspirational working classes. In many respects, modern approaches to product branding and the vast marketing industry that has developed in our own time are a continuation and elaboration of the food and drink branding phenomenon whose origins can be traced to around the time when Mrs Beeton first put pen to paper. In examining Mrs Beeton's influence on the culinary tastes of the English-speaking world, we shouldn't forget that Mrs Beeton was, and remains, something of a brand herself.

Since its early days, the food and drink industry has always been fond of using *characters* to personify their products: the usual association is with the homeliness and honest values of the character. A particularly popular fictitious brand character is Betty Crocker, who is enormously well known in the United States as a brand for the eponymous corporation that makes cake mixes and other baking products for housewives. Isabella Beeton, however, was very much real,

29

embodying certain homespun values which other real-life character brands have also embodied, such as Colonel Sanders of Kentucky Fried Chicken fame.

The rise to prominence of food brands in the mid-nineteenth century

Let's now examine in more detail how brands came to prominence in the 1840s to 1850s in the food business.

The 1840s and 1850s were generally a time of great deprivation and hunger in the United Kingdom and the United States. *A Christmas Carol*, Charles Dickens's famous story about the redemptive powers of human kindness and generosity, was published in 1843, and even at the time the significance of its publication in the midst of the "Hungry Forties" was clear.

Historians attribute the economic tribulations of the period to the migration of millions of people from the country to the town in search of work in the new factories that had sprung up as a consequence of the Industrial Revolution. The movement of huge numbers of people put enormous strain on the infrastructure (or lack of) in the towns and cities whose populations had increased so rapidly.

For many, the first effect of moving from the country to the towns was to reduce rather than increase standards of living. Just as under rationing in the Second World War country people tended to eat better than city dwellers, so people moving from country to city in the 1840s and 1850s would have taken with them memories of a rural life that, while hardly in any sense prosperous, would at least have given them the opportunity to grow some of their own food.

As the towns and cities increased in population, serious nutritional problems began to surface. This was a period before food laws. You bought your food and drink as seen, and if what you saw turned out to be something rather different from what you'd wanted, well, that was your bad luck. *Caveat emptor* was the ruling principle. After all, many suppliers of food and drink were themselves on the brink of poverty, and were prepared to go to extraordinary lengths to maximize their profit from what they were selling. If customers got a raw deal, it was simply hard cheese (sometimes literally).

Bakers, for example, got into the habit of adding powdered chalk to their flour to make it look whiter and increase its weight without actually increasing the amount of flour used. Dairies would water down the milk they sold and then add chalk powder to make it look white again. It was not unusual for toxic additives to be used. For example, Gloucester cheese was sometimes given its characteristic red hue, not by maturing it in the proper way, but by taking a cheaper cheese and augmenting it with red lead—a substance that is now known to be neuro-toxic.

Even where a food producer did not resort to such practices, the quality of hygiene in many food producers' establishments was, to put it mildly, less than what might have been expected. For example, a sample of what was hopefully described as ice cream, analyzed in London in 1881, was found to contain quite a few substances most unlikely to inspire customer loyalty, including cotton fibers, straw, human and cat hairs, fleas, lice, and bed bugs. This, though, was a comparatively mild abuse compared with the activities of one vil-lainous London chocolate manufacturer who sold children "chocolate" that was found to consist of brown paint mixed with melted candle wax.

The emergence of the product brand

At a time when lack of money meant lack of power, poorer people often had little choice but to take these gastric abominations or leave them. The middle classes, though, wanted something better, and felt they were entitled to it. In particular, they wanted to get what they paid for, they wanted guarantees of quality, and they wanted to know they were buying from a producer who observed standards of hygiene and health. Ultimately, it was this demand on the part of middle classes in the United Kingdom and the United States that led to the creation of the *brand* as a concept which has dominated food and drink production ever since.

When a rich man paid to install street lighting in a previously unlit London street, poorer people living in the street also benefited. In much the same way, the rise of brands that catered to the money-backed wishes of the emerging middle class also benefited poorer classes of society, who themselves exercised all the choice they could and increasingly preferred the "known" brands.

To the modern eye, the reason for developing a brand is obvious: it is a hallmark of a particular supplier's products and allows that sup-plier the opportunity to win the loyalty of customers who like the brand and want to keep buying it. This, however, was initially less important than the powerful motivation food producers had to offer guarantees of quality.

In the 1850s, for example, five brothers with the surname of McDougall began selling flour in the burgeoning industrial city of Manchester. Their flour became recognized for its quality and freedom from adulteration. In 1864 they invented what they described as "patent self-raising flour." They found a ready market for this flour, which, as it included raising agents, was particularly suitable for baking. The new self-raising flour was immediately popular, and along with the guarantees of quality and purity stemming from the McDougalls' reputation, its popularity brought the brothers huge commercial success.

Another popular brand in the flour industry was Brown & Polson's cornflour. This began to be produced in 1854 by John Polson, who had taken over a milling firm called Browns in 1840. Fortunately for Polson, Mrs Beeton was kind enough to mention Brown & Polson's cornflour in her recipes, and he became a millionaire as a result. Brown & Polson's cornflour is still sold in supermarkets today.

Five brothers—Charles, Leonard, Bramwell, Ernest, and Stanley Gates—were behind one of the most popular of all nineteenth-century food brands. In 1885 they decided to promote their wares by using a picture of a cow to represent the milk they offered, and a gate to represent their name. The Cow & Gate brand captured the public imagination, and the company they founded is still trading successfully today.

Many of the food and drink brands that are part of our everyday experience today have their origins in this period. Sometimes the obscurity of these origins seems strangely at odds with the fame of the brand today. For example, in 1892, after several years of experimentation, a coffee enthusiast from Nashville, Tennessee called Joel Owsley Cheek produced what he decided was absolutely the right blend of coffee. He went to the largest hotel in Nashville and persuaded the management to let him make coffee for the guests. The hotel was known as the Maxwell House Hotel, and so Maxwell House coffee came into being. Maxwell House is today one of the most successful brands of the leading international food and drink manufacturer Kraft Foods Inc.

As well as dairy products and special blends of coffee or tea (all of which, because of the risk of adulteration and generally poor quality, offered a fertile commercial arena to a producer who was offering quality from the outset), bottled sauces were also heavily branded in the nineteenth century.

There were several reasons for this. For one thing, there was an enormous demand from all classes of society for tasty sauces that improved the often bland food of the time. And making a sauce was fairly straightforward and needed only a relatively small amount of capital, yet if the sauce became successful, profits could be vast. Additionally, once the right recipe for a bottled sauce had been concocted, it could be repeated indefinitely and supplied to what we nowadays call a loyal customer base. The history of bottled sauces contains some of the earliest concerted attempts to win customers' loyalty by impressing them with a brand.

In fact, many nineteenth-century fortunes were made from bottled sauce. Often, the stronger the sauce, the more popular it was likely to be. The British Empire was proud of its possession of India, and the exotic flavors written about so evocatively in magazine stories were eagerly sampled in the homeland. Housewives and cooks hurried into their kitchens to try to replicate exotic Indian foods with whatever spices they had.

By the late nineteenth century, there were hundreds of commercially made sauces, relishes, chutneys, piccalillis (a class of sauces consisting of vegetables picked in brine, vinegar and mustard, and yellowed with powdered turmeric—nicer than it sounds), mustards, and ketchups. Many are still sold today, though not all in vast quantities. The most successful have become household names, with brand loyalty transferring easily and almost as a matter of course from generation to generation.

One of the best-known sauces of today, Worcestershire Sauce, derives from this period. It was discovered when a barrel of relish made from an Indian recipe sent in by a customer was left in the cellar of a chemist's shop in Worcester, England. It was inadvertently forgotten for many years, by which time it was well mature. Made from a well-kept recipe, and still bearing the name of the chemist's shop—Lea & Perrins—it has become one of the world's most widely used sauces.

Bottled sauce, though, is far from being a British prerogative. The famous Tabasco sauce, extremely popular in North and South America as well as in Europe, owes its origins to the American Civil War. The recipe for Tabasco is still a closely guarded secret, but its origin isn't. An American soldier fighting in the Mexican War found some pepper seeds when he was posted to the Mexican state of Tabasco. The plant had pretty flowers that he thought would look good back home in his garden in Louisiana. When he got home, he planted the seeds on an island known as Avery, just off Louisiana's coast, and owned by a wealthy local family with the same name, who were making their fortune with American's first salt mine, providing salt used to preserve meat to feed Confederate troops.

Unfortunately for the Avery family, the island was shortly afterwards taken by the Union army, and the family were forced to flee to Texas until the end of the war. Three years later, they finally managed to return, only to find their mansion looted and their plantation in ruins. Nothing remained but a crop of Tabasco peppers and some piles of salt. Fortunately for the world's palates, a son-in-law of the Avery family named Edmund McIlhenny was sensible enough to experiment by crushing the peppers and mixing them with garlic, vinegar, and salt. He aged this mixture in barrels, siphoned off the liquid, and bottled it in empty cologne bottles. The result was an exceptionally strong and piquant sauce which his friends and neighbors liked so much that he started bottling the sauce and selling it beyond his locality. Before long, it found a wider market, and it is now sold around the world.

But brandings and the quality they promised were not applied only to particular concoctions or special formulations. A prized brand could also be gained by a supplier who took the trouble to source his food or drink from a particular location. There is no better example of this than the "railway milk" produced by the London grocer John Sainsbury, which played an instrumental role in developing his shop into the chain of stores that grew into the major supermarket retailer of today.

Case study: the evolution of the grocery retailer J Sainsbury plc

John and Mary Sainsbury founded an emporium in Drury Lane, London in 1869 to supply dairy products in the West End. The small shop prospered. Strict attention to hygiene, a real awareness of what customers wanted, and a wide variety of wholesome goods were all factors in its success, but the innovative spirit of the couple played a big role too.

The railways were beginning to change the way food was supplied to the capital. Today, when we take for granted there is in London all the variety of food that life can afford (to adapt a saying of Dr Johnson's), it's easy to forget that this was by no means always the case. In the eighteenth and early nineteenth century, sheer logistical problems of distribution restricted the diet of most Londoners to ale, salted meat, bread, and the occasional tired-looking vegetable.

But by the 1860s, the use of the railway had greatly broadened the range of delicacies available to Londoners. The middle-class housewife could read *The Book of Household Management* and be confident that the often ambitious recipes contained therein were feasible, as long as she knew where to shop. The Sainsbury's stores were perfectly placed to meet the new demand for superior provisions for middle-class households, and spared no effort to deliver top-quality goods.

The Sainsburys saw that milk brought into London directly from farms in Somerset and Devon would be much better than the sorry liquid produced by cows kept in cramped and dirty conditions in London. The couple used the railways to bring in rich, creamy, well-flavored milk from the West Country—their milk became renowned as "Sainsbury's railway milk." The fame of this white nectar made the Sainsbury's shop known throughout London and brought the middle classes—or at least their servants—flocking to it.

With popularity came expansion. By 1882 there were four Sainsbury's emporia. That same year, John Sainsbury constructed his own bacon-smoking stoves. The bacon he smoked in these became the first Sainsbury's-branded product. He also decided to supply a superior range of products, which he packaged more elaborately. By 1900, the Sainsbury's chain had increased to 48 shops, every establishment still run on traditional lines, with customers coming to a counter and asking for what they wanted.

The Sainsbury's story is a useful example of how a food and drink supplier with an instinct for winning an edge over its rivals can build its business. The sale of railway milk to give customers a special quality of milk was obviously a good idea, but at the time seemed a truly original stroke of commercial acumen. Many of the challenges that Sainsbury's has faced since then have required similar creativity and commercial flair to overcome.

By 1900, John Sainsbury, despite his success, faced competition from large retailers who were moving in on the food market. To assert the quality of his shops and emphasize the Sainsbury identity, he refitted them with carefully designed tiled walls, ceramic mosaic floors, and marble-topped counters. He drafted a new rulebook to formalize trading and working practices: an early example of regulations for corporate identity standardization, familiar today to anyone who has worked in a large retailing organization.

Sainsbury's now had a distinctive shop design and product packaging, and a culture dedicated to maximizing the quality of the food on offer and overall customer service. Customers walking into any of the chain's shops would instantly recognize them as Sainsbury's.

In the 1920s, Sainsbury's created its own transport fleet to facilitate its expansion out of London—a major innovation at the time. By January 1928, when John Sainsbury died, the chain he had started was one of the UK's biggest food retailers. It went on to greater strength under his eldest son, the number of branches passing 300 by the 1920s and extending from Kent to Nottinghamshire. The chain was controlled from the company's headquarters at Blackfriars, London, where the administrative staff worked. Also at Blackfriars were the depot and a factory that produced sausages and other meat products for the branches.

In the 1950s, Sainsbury's was one of the first chains in the United Kingdom to introduce the US idea of self-service shops. A new house style was devised with checkouts, trolleys, refrigerated cabinets, fluorescent lighting, as well as a new and simplified product packaging design. During the 1950s all shops were converted to this new format.

In the 1970s, Sainsbury's responded to strikes, the oil crisis, and rising inflation by looking at new ways of becoming more efficient. New stores were built, much bigger than supermarkets of the past. This new style of store, which was already widespread in the United States, had ample parking facilities and exciting new in-store outlets such as bakeries and delicatessens. The new stores also started to sell non-food products such as hardware, cleaning materials, and household utensils. They were better suited to the lifestyles of people who wanted to pick up as much of their week's shopping in one visit and from one shop as they could.

In the 1980s and 1990s, Sainsbury's was among the first retailers to introduce various new types of technology into shops, including scanning checkouts, electronic funds transfer at point of sale (EFTPoS)—called direct debits today—computerized stock control, and sales-based ordering. It wasn't until the mid-1990s that Sainsbury's results began to deteriorate, with the organization losing much of its impetus as an innovator. It launched its loyalty card

"Reward" arguably too late, after its rivals Tesco and Safeway had already established their own loyalty cards. In April 1997 Tesco announced record profits and attributed these to its loyalty card.

Sainsbury's, which had been left behind by its rivals in the matter of loyalty cards, was determined not to be left behind in the new race among large supermarkets to move into financial services. Today, it continues to compete vigorously with its principal rival, Tesco, for a more significant share of the UK's food and financial services markets.

The growth in importance of food and drink brands during the twentieth century

As the nineteenth century reached its close, the United States took over from the United Kingdom as the leader in population and economic growth in the English-speaking world, establishing a lead in GNP that only widened as the twentieth century advanced.

The new leader in food and drink brands would henceforth be the United States; the rest of the world would follow in her footsteps. Her rapidly increasing population (it shot up from 50 million in 1880 to 76 million in 1900) created a vast and expanding market of consumers who were looking for value for money, taste sensations, and the opportunity to make a statement about the kind of people they were by choosing certain brands.

According to studies of brand reputation today, the most successful brand in the world is Coca-Cola, a brand that even in its early days assumed a cultural as well as commercial significance. Its success shows how organizations can use the right kind of branding to develop customer loyalty. The entire brand—the distinctive hand-written logo, the look of the bottles, the color of the drink (which is in fact colored simply by adding caramel, and would otherwise be a murky pale color)—helped from the beginning to win customer loyalty from customers impressed by the taste, the stimulating properties, and the association with an all-American lifestyle.

Case study: Coca-Cola—the drink and the branding

Like many successful drink brands, Coca-Cola started life as a medicinal product. The first recipe was devised by a pharmacist from Atlanta, John Pemberton, at his pharmaceutical firm, the Pemberton Chemical Company, in 1866. He and his bookkeeper, Frank

Robinson, invented the name and designed the flowing script that has become the Coca-Cola trademark. The name came from two of the active ingredients: cocaine extracted from the coca leaf, and the caffeine-rich extracts of the Cola nut. With these ingredients, the drink soon acquired a reputation for its powerful stimulating and analgesic effects.

Robinson's method of marketing his drink has continued to this day. He did not bottle the drink himself, but simply sold the syrup to local soda fountains that would bottle it and serve it to customers. Supported by advertising that was innovative from the beginning, the drink became enormously successful. A succession of takeovers led to the formation of the Coca-Cola Company, which continued to grow in strength and after the Second World War made a variety of acquisitions that introduced new soft drinks to the market it had in some senses created.

Ultimately, brandings in the food and drink industry are designed to ensure the consumer buys the product repeatedly, knowing it will always taste the same and give the same pleasure it gave when the customer sampled it for the first time. Consequently, the standardization of the formula or recipe is enormously important, and even highly successful organizations have come unstuck when seeking to alter the brand's taste.

A classic example is Coca-Cola itself. In 1985 the then chief executive of Coca-Cola, Roberto C. Goizueta, introduced a new taste—branded "New Coke"—for the flagship drink. The taste was popular in tests, but was met with horror when it hit the marketplace. Customers begged for the return of the old formula. On 11 July 1985, a mere 79 days after the launch of "New Coke," the public outcry over the loss of their favorite drink obliged Coca-Cola to bring back what was immediately rebranded as "Classic Coke." "New Coke" remained as a brand, but it has never caught on. Today it is known as "Coke II," but is available only in the United States in a few city areas. Outside the United States, the new formula never took off at all, and most non-US customers are probably completely unaware of the existence of Coke II.

This incident shows that when a brand reaches a certain critical mass it is "owned" as much by the people who buy it as by the organization that makes it. This is customer loyalty in action.

The success of the Coca-Cola brand is seen not only in the iconic status it has achieved in many countries as an emblem of US capitalism, but also in its impact on many aspects of culture. The drinking of Coca-Cola by a character in a movie, for example, would be taken by the audience to indicate something about the character, probably connected with youth, vitality, and energy.

Case study: Kellogg's Cornflakes

Another successful loyalty-inspiring branding, which originated from a product designed to improve health, is Kellogg's Cornflakes, one of the earliest and still among the most popular breakfast cereals. In 1900, two brothers who had a profound interest in the embryonic science of nutrition founded the Sanitas Food Company to market crunchy, tasty flakes of processed grain.

Throughout the nineteenth century, as Mrs Beeton's book shows, breakfast was simply a form of lunch or dinner that took place earlier in the day. It was routine for nineteenth century gentlemen to start the day with steak, potatoes, devilled kidneys, and a variety of hot, spicy meat-based dishes.

The Kellogg brothers believed this diet was extremely harmful to health; the poor condition of the patients who came for rest cures at the "sanatorium" they set up at Battle Creek, Michigan, seemed to confirm this. They were convinced that toasted wheat and corn products were much healthier, especially in the morning. Until 1922, the brothers made only cornflakes, but then began producing other cereals. They played a big role in creating the popular fashion of starting the day with cereals rather than more elaborate meals, and today the brand they created is regarded as extremely trustworthy, a hallmark of good quality. The brand is associated in customers' minds with concepts of homeliness, trustworthiness, good taste, and healthfulness. Like Coca-Cola, Kellogg's cornflakes are a familiar product in many households.

Case study: Skippy peanut butter

One big difference between the branding of food and drink in the nineteenth and twentieth centuries is that nineteenth-century brands tended to stamp an individual name on a generic type of food or drink, while in the twentieth century there was more focus on inventing identities for completely new types of food or drink products. One food product that has remained generic while being the subject of ferocious branding campaigns by many producers is peanut butter.

The peanut is a highly concentrated food. Pound for pound, peanuts have more protein, minerals, and vitamins than beef liver. The peanut also contains more fat, weight for weight, than double cream, and more food energy (calories) than sugar. In most peanut-growing countries, the peanut is used mainly for its edible oil. But in the United States, more than half the harvested crop is ground into peanut butter, with much of the rest sold as roasted and salted nuts or for use in candy and bakery products. Perhaps the most successful peanut butter brand in the world today is Skippy peanut butter.

Peanut butter as we know it today was invented in 1890 by a St Louis physician who wanted to give his patients an easily digestible high-protein food. But the idea of crushing peanuts into a paste and using them as a spread had occurred to many before then. Peanuts were known as long ago as 950 BC and originally came from South America. The ancient Incas enjoyed peanuts and made them into a kind of paste-like substance. The great American chemist and food technician, George Washington Carver, saw the potential of crushed peanuts as a foodstuff, but didn't patent the idea or seek to develop it because he believed food products were a gift from God.

The Skippy brand began in 1932. Its owners cleverly helped its evolution along, winning it a high profile by sponsoring popular television shows and ensuring that they became associated with the Skippy brand. In 1963, Skippy peanut butter was immortalized in illustrations by the enormously popular artist Norman Rockwell, while US celebrities advertised the product on television and generally promoted it, as they did Coca-Cola, as an essential part of a healthy American lifestyle.

The success of these US brands came about rapidly because of what they offered customers in terms of taste, impact, fashion, and positive lifestyle associations. A brand that is famous today in many parts of the world outside the United States, but had to win its fame more arduously, is Marmite.

Case study: Marmite

Marmite (French for the kind of pot in which stews and casseroles are cooked) is a brand name given today to a particular recipe of extract of brewer's yeast, a substance whose only function is to ferment sugars into alcohol. For many years this by-product of the brewing process was regarded as a nuisance rather than a potentially valuable food source, but further investigation revealed it could be made into a concentrated food product that resembled meat extract in appearance, smell, and color, but obviously contained no meat.

In 1902, the Marmite Food Company was founded in Burton-on-Trent (England) in order to exploit the commercial possibilities of yeast extract. It had perfected a recipe with an appealing taste and smell, and the food had popular appeal at a time when many people ate inadequate and unhealthy food and had little money to spend on nourishment. Marmite would be seen as a cheap and wholesome addition to their diet—or so the company hoped.

Unlike some food brands, Marmite was not an instant success, but the good deal offered in terms of taste, nourishment, and cost eventually conquered the unadventurous palate of the UK public. Marmite became an increasingly popular spread for toast, as well as an instant nourishing drink (simply add a few teaspoonfuls to a mug of boiling water).

The discovery of vitamins in 1912 was a big boon. The manufacturers were quick to point out that the sticky black foodstuff was an excellent source of B vitamins. This hugely increased demand for Marmite from hospitals, schools, and institutions of all kinds, with many tons of the stuff dispatched to war-torn countries overseas during the First World War and then again in the Second World War. Particularly during the Second World War, Marmite filled an important niche as a light and portable source of nourishment which reminded soldiers of home. And with its vitamin content, Marmite helped to combat outbreaks of nutritional diseases such as beriberi.

Since then, Marmite has continued to grow in popularity, and today is one of the most widely recognized brands in the kitchen. Clever design of the Marmite pot and the straightforward and slightly old-fashioned appearance of the logo have contributed to this popularity. It is a remarkable success story, especially as, if you think about it, there is something rather odd about finding in kitchens a branded version of a highly specialized by-product of the brewing process. Many habitual consumers of Marmite still believe it is a meat extract. Funnily enough, when Marmite was first sold commercially, the manufacturers underplayed its vegetarian nature, whereas today, when vegetarian lifestyles are more popular, Marmite is promoted heavily as a vegetarian product and important source of nutrition for that kind of diet. Again, the link between a successful food branding and health or, strictly speaking, perception of healthiness, is an intimate and important one.

Developments in customer loyalty since the nineteenth century

As investigators into the nature of customer loyalty, we need to be willing to travel into the more recent past as well as into the nineteenth century. It might reasonably be asked what insights into customer loyalty can be gleaned from looking into the more recent past.

While it is certainly abundantly reasonable to regard the nineteenth century as the century when product brands rose to prominence and when they tended to dominate commercial life, it would be a mistake to imagine that there was suddenly an end to this trend on January 1, 1901: the first day of the twentieth century.

In fact, the domination of product brands in commercial life in general and in the business-to-consumer world in particular persisted until surprisingly recently. Even as late as the 1970s, most prominent brands were still product brands, and indeed many had become established in the previous century. Consumers did make use of brands in areas such as financial services, insurance, travel, and so on—brands we would nowadays tend to regard as service brands. However, these brands were usually purchased in a face-to-face transaction in a retail outlet (such as a bank branch or a travel agency), and any post-purchase service provided with them would usually have also been provided via the outlet (for example, facilities connected with the day-to-day running of a bank account). There were no remote service facilities in this period; it was generally possible to phone one's branch for example in order to talk to one's bank manager, but the whole modern notion of extensive and comprehensive service being supplied remotely had not yet developed.

What was happening to service brands at this time?

There was a gradual rise in the importance of service as an element of brands in the period immediately after the Second World War, but really significant progress was only made in the 1960s, which saw the rise to prominence of self-service in retail food marketing and in banking. At about the same time, consumers started to become aware of their power, and consumer rights became an important talking point, especially in the United States.

The rise of service issues in marketing to consumers was much increased and spurred on by technological developments. These developments have included the invention of the microchip (which eventually made for compact, portable, and extremely high-power computers) and of course the introduction of the Internet.

The result is that today, remotely-supplied service is not only intimately connected with service brands, but is also continuing to grow in importance. So many organizations deliver services remotely nowadays rather than via bricks-and-mortar outlets that town centers no longer have many types of outlets they once featured; such as the retail shops of utilities companies, which have been eliminated from High Streets.

Let us now travel in time from the past and into the present, with the second core principle of this book firmly in our minds: that organizations succeed in winning customer loyalty by attuning themselves to the key social developments of the environment in which they are operating, and by doing their best to forecast future trends.

Conclusion

In this chapter, which has focused on the past, we have correspondingly focused on certain examples of product brands because the social and economic conditions of the nineteenth century were especially conducive to the rise of reliable products. However, many of the lessons we can learn from how product brands rose to prominence in the nineteenth century are also highly relevant to the subject of service brands, which are the kind of brands we mainly concern ourselves with in this book. The most important lessons are:

- Brands win customer loyalty directly by establishing a recognizable product (or service) on which the promotional "dialog" between seller and customer can focus.
- Brands establish the "permission of the marketplace" with customers by offering clear and genuine benefits.
- A good brand is based on a solid and honest offering to the customer. One factor that seems undeniably common to all successful brands is the *genuineness* of the brand's quality, or the fact that the product represented by the brand has something special about it.
- For brands, as with art, survival is perhaps the best and most reliable test of ultimate quality.

- A good brand is supported from the outset by positive marketing associations and is consciously developed to become part of a consumer's lifestyle. Consider the associations of Coca-Cola and the way it is seen as a US icon and a celebration of friendship, comradeship, and youth instead of just as a brown fizzy sugary drink in a bottle. The "brown fizzy sugary drink in a bottle" is a dispassionate, objective, description before the catalyst of product marketing has worked its magic.
- If a brand can start by portraying itself as unique and special, it is off to a flying start. A good brand will be able to create its own market, in much the same way as Coca-Cola did.

This chapter has looked at how the changing conditions of society have influenced opportunities to win customer loyalty by offering customers things they really want, and continue to want. These are things, furthermore, that more and more customers want. These insights into how this process has worked in the past advances our overall theme. This is the core argument: to identify ways of winning customer loyalty we need to be a kind of time traveler, understanding the changing conditions of society as someone who was traveling in time and observing these changes as an outsider might.

Having considered the changing conditions of society in the past, let us now look at the changing conditions of society in the *present*. Yes, product brands remain extremely important, when increasingly, it is not product brands organizations are trying to market, but *services* and *service brands*. Furthermore, it is in the area of service brands that for many organizations the greatest amount of potential competitive edge is nowadays waiting to be won.

Appendix

When we were writing this book, we mentioned the project to a friend and he said, "Oh, so I suppose you will be writing about Green Shield stamps."

Well, as you see, we *aren't* writing about Green Shield stamps, at least not to any significant extent.

Why not? The reason is, quite simply, that essentially loyalty-winning gimmicks such as Green Shield stamps, cigarette coupons (which allowed you to acquire various supposedly desirable consumer goods in direct proportion to the fatal damage you were doing to your body), Air Miles, and so on, are not really subtle ways of engineering genuine, authentic customer loyalty, but instead fundamentally insincere incentives (gimmicks) whereby the organization aims to obtain loyalty from a customer on a sort of bribed basis. The idea is that the customer would not perhaps want to confer the loyalty were it not for the bribe.

Customer loyalty cards seem, at least superficially, more "respectable" than trading stamps—perhaps if for no other reason than that customer loyalty cards bear some resemblance to bank cards or credit cards—but really they are no more than a slightly more sophisticated version of trading stamps.

Customer loyalty cards continue to be popular, but the evidence suggests that what customers really prefer are lower prices, at least in the intensely competitive marketplaces in which customer loyalty cards are usually offered (such as supermarket food shopping). Any organization offering customer loyalty cards is bound to ask itself at some point what real evidence there is that the loyalty cards actually *do* win any loyalty. While it is never easy to prove this either way, there is a general sense in the customer loyalty "profession" that the future of winning customer loyalty does not lie in gimmicks or loyalty cards, but in creating better relationships between organizations and their customers. This is, of course, exactly what this book is all about.

In the meantime, since this particular chapter focuses particularly on time travel, here is a timeline showing some of the customer loyalty gimmicks that have been tried since 1958.

- *1958* The Green Shield Trading Stamp business is founded by Richard Tompkins in the United Kingdom. Tompkins is inspired by similar schemes in the United States.
- *1960s and 1970s* Consumers receive green or pink stamps with their shopping, and glasses with their petrol.
- *1965* Co-op launches dividend stamps.
- *1977* Tesco abandons Green Shield stamps. Tesco says it believes its customers prefer lower prices to the chance to collect trading stamps.
- *1980* Banks use new technology to foster "relationship banking."
- *1988* Air Miles Travel Promotions founded.
- *1993* Sainsbury's Homebase launches Spend & Save card. Boots begins planning a loyalty card.
- *1994* Asda introduces limited loyalty card scheme.

- *1995* Tesco launches Clubcard—dismissed by David Sainsbury as a return to Green Shield stamps. Sainsbury's introduces a Reward card and Safeway enters the market with the ABC card.
- *1996* Tesco creates a student Clubcard and a card for mothers.
- *1997* W H Smith launches Clubcard, Boots launches Advantage Card, Tesco adds full range of financial services, and McDonald's launches its first card—the McExtra Card.
- *1998* Tesco offers electricity and telecommunications. The CWS Dividend Card replaces Co-op stamps.
- *1999* Asda discontinues its loyalty scheme to focus on a Rollback campaign. Boots launches the Advantage loyalty credit card in conjunction with Egg. "Advantage Point" goes into Boots stores. Tesco launches Clubcard Deals, which enable customers to use their vouchers to obtain discounts on travel and leisure products.
- *2000* Safeway drops the 7 million strong ABC card, saying, "Our customers don't want a relationship with us."
- *2002* Nectar card launched by Air Miles founder Keith Mills. Somerfield pilots a Saver Card.
- *2003* Vodafone joins Nectar. Barclaycard's switch from Air Miles to Nectar points causes complaints. 50 percent of UK households have a Nectar card (11 million out of 22 million). 85 percent of UK households have at least one loyalty card. Marks & Spencer falls foul of the Office of Fair Trading (OFT) over the launch of its credit card.
- *2004* Somerfield launches a Saver Card.

3 New customers, new challenges

The way businesses have served their customers in the emerging consumer markets of the nineteenth century and through time to the present day have a great deal to teach us. But as time travelers seeking insights into customer loyalty, we need to plunder the present for these insights, too, especially when the present is the product of as much tumultuous recent change as ours.

In 1993, in his book *Post Capitalist Society*, Peter Drucker observed:

> *Every few hundred years in Western history there occurs a sharp transformation. Within a few short decades, society rearranges itself—its worldview; its basic values; its social and political structure; its arts; its key institutions. Fifty years later there is a new world.*

He is describing a vast change in the fabric of an age. But he is not writing of historical events. The age is *our* age; he argues that we are living today through the kind of transformation he describes.

Identifying and defining fundamental changes in society that are going on now is always more difficult than writing history, which—by definition—affords us the benefit of hindsight. Our remit in this chapter—to show how today's changes are affecting customer behavior—is demanding. We have to try to understand how current trends and developments are affecting society so that organizations whose commercial goal is to win, impress, and retain customers today can do so. Organizations desperately want to achieve these objectives, and to do so better than their competition.

Drucker's argument is now widely accepted. Every day in the modern business world, it is generally believed, competition gets tougher—thanks to new economic pressures, new markets, technological innovation, rapid scientific advance, and increased cross-border competition. These forces drive the social changes that create new kinds of customer demand, and these new kinds of demand in turn influence the way we live our lives (the "24-hour society" for example).

A nineteenth-century model for winning customer loyalty

In the boom in product brands in the early nineteenth century, suppliers tried to win customer loyalty by meeting basic concerns about safety, consistency, and quality. The McDougall brothers, for example, sold their flour on its purity, consistency, and wholesomeness. It was only much later—in the 1970s—that they advertised their flour as "super-sifted" to distinguish its quality from that of rivals. Today, everyday commodities are routinely promoted as chic, status-conferring luxury goods. Witness a recent *Forbes* article about "Salt chic" (*Forbes*, October 28, 2002), featuring a Californian restaurant chef using 20 varieties of gourmet sodium chloride, with a certain variety of Japanese sea salt costing US$45 per kilo.

By the end of the nineteenth century, food regulation in the United Kingdom—and laws regulating the quality of other products—meant the consumer could increasingly take it for granted that most organizations would be offering a quality product. Product advertising shifted away from testimonials of quality towards high-status endorsements from aristocratic and Royal households and associations with famous things or persons. (For example, numerous businesses whose goods were being used on the ship advertised the fact before the maiden voyage of the *Titanic* in 1912.)

But the desire for basic quality is only the starting point and necessary condition for customer demand. Once quality is assured, loyalty derives from elsewhere. Especially important is the desire to acquire social status through one's buying choices. Throughout history, the desire to establish social status has been a significant driving force behind consumption of goods and services.

In today's buying world, it's probably fair to say many customers feel they already have everything they *need*, at least at a fundamental physical level. Yet the very fact that there is so much competitiveness among organizations who are selling what appear—on the face of it—to be similar products and services suggests that even when people are buying things they believe they need, they have motives other than the mere need to acquire essentials.

But what are these motives? What are customers most concerned about receiving from organizations? The answer is simple, but momentous. The factor most likely to influence customers' buying decisions, when they are buying things available from a large number of organizations, is *the quality of service the organizations are offering*.

Increasingly, products come "bound up" with a level of service that is the decisive factor in winning competitive advantage for that product. As time travelers looking at the changing nature of customer loyalty over time, we shall find that focusing on changing attitudes towards service can yield us invaluable insights with massive financial implications in today's markets where winning customer loyalty is so important.

A brief history of time travel

Nowadays, when an organization wants to do something more effectively, it often starts by convening a "focus group" of its staff or customers or users. A focus group is a group of people who collectively answer detailed questions about their behavior, tastes, motivations, and so on. Ever since a focus group advised Bill Clinton to wear a "red power tie" when seeking re-election, they have been a fruitful source of humor, but they have their uses too.

They are most often used by businesses wanting to know what their customers want. It's interesting to speculate what we might learn if we could travel back through time 150 years to a focus group of the nineteenth-century customers whose needs and priorities we discussed in the previous chapter.

Back then, the average customer had a vastly lower income and a significantly inferior standard of living to that enjoyed by his or her counterpart today. Their ideas of essentials and indeed luxuries were very different from ours. Yet despite the big differences between consumers of the past and consumers today, we are likely to draw the surprising conclusion from our nineteenth-century focus group that many nineteenth-century customers would actually have been *more demanding* about service than we are today.

In the nineteenth century, he who paid the piper really did call the tune. Capital was scarce. All kinds of money were scarce. Most ways of earning a living gave little reward other than subsistence-level existence. The idea that you might accumulate wealth from waged or salaried income was a non-starter in the nineteenth century for most occupations. Even the enormously popular and furiously hard-working Charles Dickens (1812—1870) remained under financial pressure for most of his life; it was only towards the end of his career, when he gave a series of spectacularly successful readings in the United States, that he made enough money to enable him to leave £98 000—perhaps £3 million at today's prices—when he died. The rich in the nineteenth century tended to be those who had inherited it from wealthy ancestors. Only a few were self-made.

It was a buyer's market. True, only a small part of the population—perhaps about 5 percent—had any real buying power in the sense of being able to choose between suppliers and feeling entitled to be courted by them. Today, in the more prosperous society of the early twenty-first century, perhaps 90 percent of the population has sufficient buying power to make choices between suppliers and to feel entitled to be *served*.

Yet just because more of the population feels this entitlement today than felt it in, say, 1850, does not mean that fundamental attitudes and expectations of service have changed since then. They haven't. Demands for service reflect our fundamental needs as human beings, and nineteenth-century consumers were in fact even more demanding on this front than we are today.

In particular, Victorian consumers not only *hoped* for the following from their suppliers, but would have taken for granted that they were entitled to these things:

- They expected suppliers to know them and their personal requirements and spare no effort in meeting those needs.
- In particular, they expected suppliers to be thoroughly acquainted with their likes and dislikes.
- They expected performance to be completely reliable.
- They expected impeccable courtesy.
- They expected suppliers to be knowledgeable and helpful.
- Generally, they expected service providers—if we might call them by a modern term—to show promptness, eagerness, and a readiness to make helpful suggestions.

But what kind of service do modern consumers want? On the face of it, their requirements are shaped by the nature of the economy today. In particular, capital is no longer scarce, although in an age of—possibly—excessive personal borrowing, good credit records may be. And we have a more egalitarian society in which people are no longer prepared to play lowly and subservient roles deferring to their "betters" as was perhaps the case in the past.

In this society, the motivation to provide good service is more complex than it was in the nineteenth century. There is no longer the likelihood of starvation if you fail to earn a living; the penalty for being inactive economically is certainly a constrained financial existence, but hardly the ghastly poverty that blighted so many nineteenth-century lives. A nineteenth-century butcher's boy who was insolent to a customer would probably have been sacked without a "character" (as references used to be called). The absence of a character could make it impossible to find a new job.

Today, we do not fear the sack as much as we did. Furthermore, because people no longer regard themselves as inherently inferior in social status to anybody else, they are less likely to feel *obliged* to serve certain people. So why, in today's society, should anybody want to offer good service at all?

Ultimately, it depends on partly personal inclination and a motivating work environment that convinces its people of the fundamental importance of service to the business's success. As Archie Norman—the former head of the UK supermarket group ASDA (now part of the global supermarket group Wal-Mart)—once said, the retail supermarket business is first and foremost a service business, and if you want to do well at it, you need to hire people who basically *like* other people.

Positive, life-affirming, optimistic people are attractive, and their outlook is often contagious. They achieve great results, and why wouldn't they? They're a joy to interact with! Whether they're waiting on your table, checking you in at the hotel, repairing your computer, writing you a check for your new mortgage, selling you a new network, or solving a billing problem at your credit card company, they can make a genuine difference in the quality of your life in that moment if they treat you with a positive, up-beat, and can-do attitude.

Nobody can be motivated through money or fear of the sack to *like* people, let alone to *like serving* people. Some highly successful and productive people don't especially like other people and are happiest working in a kind of shell where they can do their own thing, pursue their own agenda, and have minimal contact with others. We probably all know a few of these characters. Many great scientists have been like this and have still achieved, ironically perhaps, a great deal for humankind; great writers, artists, and composers may also be like that. But if people who don't really like other people are working with your customers, there'll be problems. A key difference then and now is the pride a person takes in providing great service.

In the customer loyalty business we need people who do get an inherent pleasure out of giving service and who do like other people. What customers really want are not insincere servile grovellers, but *people who will take a personal interest in them and their concerns.* Inherent personal inclination is a crucial factor in whether or not it happens and the feelings that customers have as a result. Of course people can be trained to be better at customer service, but to truly excel at impressing customers, there needs to be some basic talent and inclination to help others in place from the beginning.

At the award-winning Greek bank, Egnatia Bank, Christa Fillinis, assistant director of phone banking, and Stella Stavropoulou, director of marketing, attribute their success to their human resources. They are highly motivated and highly qualified: half have first degrees and 14 percent have postgraduate qualifications. There is a lot to be said about motivating customer service staff, and we say a lot about it here in *Customer Loyalty: a guide for time travelers,* but there needs to be something to work on if the motivational initiative is going to succeed.

Modern expectations of customer service

What do modern consumers expect from customer service? Human nature doesn't change, so it's no surprise that the modern consumer would like to enjoy what his or her nineteenth-century counterparts would have expected. Unfortunately, today's customer is unlikely to have anything like the confidence of the nineteenth-century customer that she will get what she wants.

In the nineteenth century, if your grocer's boy was impolite when he delivered the week's groceries, you would simply report him to his boss and he would be sacked forthwith, to be replaced by a boy who had more sense. But any consumer today who expects impeccable politeness may be setting him or herself up for disappointment.

Again, can a modern consumer realistically expect a vendor to be thoroughly acquainted with his other likes and dislikes? The consumer would certainly find this gratifying, but would hardly take it for granted. As for organizations being completely reliable, dependable, helpful, full of constructive suggestions, and prompt in what they deliver, these again would doubtless be gratifying to modern consumers, but they wouldn't expect to find it in every case.

In essence, our service expectations today are a diluted version of those of the past. They are diluted because our expectations are—

perhaps sadly—less ambitious. But in principle we, too, want to enjoy all the following customer benefits:

- We should like our suppliers to know us and our personal requirements and to spare no effort in meeting those needs.
- In particular, we should like organizations to be thoroughly acquainted with our likes and dislikes.
- We should like organizations to be completely reliable.
- We should like service providers to show impeccable courtesy.
- We should like organizations to be dependable, helpful, and ready to make suggestions.
- Generally, we should like organizations to be prompt and eager to serve us.

Modern organizations can learn a great deal from Victorian demands. Failing to provide service experiences that customers appreciate—with characteristics that essentially have not changed for at least 150 years—is a bit sad and pathetic, but it's the reason why many customers continue resignedly to shop around.

Why the service ethic has deteriorated

Some elderly people never tire of telling you that today's quality of service is not what it was.

In many respects they are right: personal service is more difficult to get nowadays than it was in the past, mainly because far more people are candidates for service than they ever were in the past. Even in the 1930s, most people did not have bank accounts, for example, and were too poor to be significant as consumers. In both the United Kingdom and the United States, the Second World War ushered in a more egalitarian and socially democratic society in which people felt there was no reason why *they* shouldn't have the best. The old idea that only the aristocracy who had inherited their money deserved to enjoy the best from a material perspective, was dead, or dying.

However, in today's economies the people who serve customers are no more inherently inclined to give good service than they ever were, indeed they are probably less so. Generally, perhaps related to the rise of a more egalitarian society, there is perceived to be a decline in a service ethic: the notion that serving others should be a source of pride. Despite this potential problem, many organizations have successfully achieved a level of service which customers may describe as good or even very good—yet these organizations still do not retain customers, let alone win their loyalty. Why?

Because even "very good" levels of service, if they do not connect with the customers' emotional needs, do not impress. For organizations wishing to win a competitive edge by attracting more customer loyalty than their rivals, this has to be the goal. But how to make it so?

Unfortunately, there are other factors making the provision of impressive service more difficult: We live in a fast-moving consumer society; a culture and climate where business operates at a faster level, across more delivery channels, where consumers have more choice and organizations more potential customers, than was ever the case in the past.

Consider the case of Tesco, the UK's leading supermarket with over 14 million customers each week. Tesco Telecoms is the fourth retail service offered by Tesco; tesco.com is already the largest online grocer in the world and Tesco Personal Finance has signed up nearly 4 million customers in just five years. Tesco's core purpose is to create value for customers to earn their lifetime loyalty. Sir Terry Leahy, the chief executive of Tesco plc, puts it like this:

> *What creates loyalty is how much we understand your life, and what we do about it that helps your life.*

In the past, customers' lives were considerably improved by reliable products, some of which through quality and brand marques were able to win lifetime, even generational loyalty. Can service businesses do the same and provide experiences that impress customers by helping them live their lives? Let's start by looking at what's going on in customers' lives.

Trends and fads and their impact on customer demand

For our analysis, we distinguish between a trend and a fad. Fads are *ephemeral enthusiasms*. They are impossible to predict, being short term and caused by a sudden popular *whim*. Who could have predicted pet rocks, hot pants, or ponytails for men? (Fashions, of course, are merely cyclical fads—there is a more predictable regularity with which red lipstick becomes de rigueur and hemlines wax and wane, but there's no great rhyme or reason to it.)

By contrast, social trends are changes in individual behavior that are manifest in a large amount of the population. Social trends affect the way we live and the way we work. Examples are the desire to work from home, rebalancing work/life, and our emerging willingness to recycle. When a trend persists for many years, the chances are it has passed into the culture and become the norm.

There is no hard and fast way of distinguishing a social trend from an economic one. The ageing population, growing racial diversity, and decline in educational standards could be considered social trends, but of course, such trends have economic consequences as well as causing *other* social or consumer trends that are relevant to service businesses.

Funnily enough, trendspotting has itself become a trend. It's possible to register as a "trendspotter" on any number of websites. There has been an explosion in the number of "futurists" (and fortune tellers and mediums, come to that) that belies the sense of chaos that drastic social transformation brings for individuals and businesses. At the corporate level there is widespread adoption of trendspotting by companies such as Wal-Mart, Campbell's Soup, Lego, Marks & Spencer, Virgin, and ICI, who all use trend forecasting to anticipate what their customers will want in the future and guide innovation.

Even the greetings card giant Hallmark has an in-house trendspotter who apparently monitors the social milieu to spot trends as they emerge and tracks existing trends as they climb, peak, and wane. Apparently she reads virtually every new book and article on social change. If this much effort goes into greetings card manufacture, anyone running a service business should be in a cold sweat by now (though what's the betting the best-selling cards are still the ones "left blank for your own message"?).

Why is this happening? Many business leaders have lost confidence in traditional consumer research, especially when applied to innovation. This ties into a general acceleration of business processes of innovation and service delivery. Yet nonetheless there is also the belief that, in the information age, we should be able to predict what's going to happen next. Companies are therefore constantly looking for new ways to ensure that they don't become the victims of change.

Trends can be relatively easy to spot if you keep your eyes and ears open. They can give a strategic framework for innovation and help organizations keep existing products and services relevant. But just being aware of trends—developing and otherwise—is not always enough. For a service business the real challenge is to understand the choices that such trends will lead customers to make. This is how you'll get customers and then keep them.

The driver of change

Trends happen for a reason, and one of the biggest impacts on social and consumer trends is what's going on in the economy. But ask leading economists to define today's "New Economy," and it soon becomes clear that there are as many definitions as there are economists. So what is the New Economy, and how will it change our lives?

Analysts have identified three distinct economic movements that have shaped the last 150 years. From 1850 to 1918, commodities such as cotton, iron, and steel drove the economy. During this time, the new railways and factories were beginning to package work into "jobs," where workers earned wages and were accountable for the completion of specific tasks. However, the idea of working for wages had not yet rooted itself in society. Many workers still prized their traditional crafts and the interweaving of their home life and work life.

By 1918, industry was transformed by Henry Ford's vision of bringing the automobile to the masses. His new manufacturing techniques increased production to levels never thought possible, and spawned a period of unprecedented industrial expansion. The concept of "job" was perfected during this era, as workers performed specific tasks and duties that accelerated output on the production line. In this era of mass production, the growing infrastructure such as roads, airports, and telephones was a visible sign of economic growth.

In the last 20 years, industrial shifts have occurred so quickly that many economists have been at a loss to understand them. We now live in such complexity that we have had to develop whole new theories just to be able to ask the right questions. The New Economy is difficult to define. Innovations in communications technology and the globalization of trade (enabled by technology) have slowly shifted industry from the production line to industries whose major product is knowledge itself. Our concept of a job is also changing. In the industrial age the job was a certain kind of work, defined by a job description, which met the needs of the relatively slow-moving factories. Now, in a world wired together by electronic data, today's organizations need to respond more quickly to developments or be left behind by global competitors. Today's job is becoming "something we do" (a set of skills and competencies) instead of "something we are or have" (a function).

The growth of this New Economy is also hard to measure because we cannot see its infrastructure of satellites, fiber optics, and radio frequencies. In the New Economy, people are increasingly working with information and ideas and, in service businesses, their emotions, rather than with their hands. It has meant that now, as never before, people are the basic source of economic strength and growth—not land or natural resources. Look at the services that are increasingly traded globally in a way that would have been unthinkable even 20 years ago: software programming, back-office services, product design, research and development, and of course customer services. Right now customers from the West are flying to developing nations for dentistry and plastic surgery.

We now have an "office economy" characterized by high-tech communications and a service orientation that has replaced the factories and product-driven focus of the industrial movement. In this world of competing service economies, the need to increase productivity (efficiency) and effectiveness will become increasingly important.

The drive for efficiency may be already well underway, yet the drive for effectiveness has hardly begun. It's already clear that to best serve customers, it's important to understand their needs, characteristics, habits, and concerns. In the course of our client research over recent years, we've identified a range of significant individual behaviors that are sufficiently prevalent among many to be called trends relevant to service businesses. We have named them as follows:

1. Interconnected individualism.
2. The permanent hurry.
3. The trust implosion.
4. Ethic-quette.
5. Rude rage.
6. Stressfulness of choice.
7. Authenticity addiction.

Interconnected individualism

Globalization has had its homogenizing effects, but paradoxically, it has also created a fragmented and diverse society—in lifestyles, in religions, in social and political allegiances. The information age has brought us an unparalleled awareness of ourselves and each other. The world is becoming more cosmopolitan and more insular at the same time; accelerating global trade, awareness, and travel coincide with intensifying local, national, ethnic, and religious identity. For governments it has created a renewed interest in ethnic, national, and cultural affinities that magnify the differences among people perhaps more than their similarities. For businesses it marks an age of niche markets, specialization, and personalization of products and services.

Fragmentation in society has led to a destruction or downsizing of traditional social networks, such as the family, leaving room for more ephemeral forms of interaction and influence. In his 2004 book *Karaoke Capitalism*, the Swedish management guru Kjell Nordstrom suggests that soon, 60 percent of households in many Western cities will be single-person. Human beings, though, are social animals, and although we may be increasingly fragmented in our living and working arrangements, there is overwhelming evidence of our need to interact, frequently and fluently. Technology has expanded our ability to share our thoughts and feelings not only with friends and family, but now more or less globally at little or no cost. Forrester Research estimate that 60 percent of online Europeans now connect with others in mutual interest or support groups. Look at the apparently increasing desire to "blog." A blog ("web log") is an online diary or journal, a web page that can be used for instant online publishing by opinion writers, part-time poets, critics, or boosters, and by family and friends, educators, clubs, or businesses—anyone with the desire to share. The blog site creates opportunities to exchange ideas, share timely news, record events, update projects, show pictures, or post writings similar to a diary or journal. It's a source of recommendation or criticism with potentially global reach.

Consider too, the emerging trend of "Twinsumerism," where customers looking for the best, the first, the most relevant to them are influenced by and listen to their taste "twins"—other individuals somewhere in the world who think, react, enjoy, and consume the way they do. Increasingly, websites that provide the opportunity to review or recommend products and services are encouraging their reviewers to add personal profiles, allowing the concept of Twinsumerism to blossom.

And what about Podcasting? There is a fast-growing band of "podcasters"—mostly amateur program makers whose radio shows are designed to be heard on iPods and other MP3 players. Since iPodder software first allowed listeners to download their favorite shows automatically, hundreds of new advertisement-free radio channels have emerged in cyberspace. At current reckoning, there may be 4 million iPods out there, but soon there will be hard discs on hundreds of millions of phones—each a potential storage device for the latest episodes of these guy-in-a-basement programs. "Podcasting creates the opportunity to talk about whatever's on your mind, without having to satisfy some great commercial entity," explains one Podcaster, ironically an advertising executive by day whose shows appear at theovernightscape.com. He describes the podcasting phenomenon as "being part of a cultural revolution. This must be what it felt like to be a hippy in the sixties." Beware big business, man.

Our desire to interact, to form allegiances and communities—real or virtual—is part of human nature. Our society has created the opportunity for many such allegiances to be formed in a few hours on the Internet. This is just the beginning, as the digital generation will be the first group of consumers to grow up with all these new tools and peer-to-peer options for communicating about their experiences—and preferences.

The generation that's coming are keen to share their experiences because many of the traditional means of corporate communication and marketing are sufficiently individualized to provide customers with the personalized, niche service and information they desire. Plus, these customers are increasingly unimpressed by traditional (producer) power and authority, wise to self-promotion, and want to hear what other customers really think of a product or service before they jump in.

With the massed technology of the information age, it should of course be possible to give customers the *individualized relationships* they want, and we know, customers have been looking for this since business began. A friend of ours, who has been shaving his head for the last 15 years, recently received a free gift "specially selected for him" from his online supermarket. What was it? Shampoo.

Of course many organizations lag behind this important customer desire because their systems are organized around the products customers hold, not the needs those customers have. But here's a quick tip from Trendwatching.com for those who have yet to restructure their databases:

The art of "Googling" (checking people's backgrounds on the Internet via search engine Google)—which started out as a useful tool for weeding out psychopaths from the online dating game—will soon be an integral part of corporate 1:1 marketing strategies. With consumers disclosing their most intimate secrets online (voluntarily!), Google has essentially created a "domestic database," i.e. a world-wide database loaded with your customers' details and profiles, with

*a depth of information your company's database can only dream of.
So instead of consumers Googling you before they buy your services,
you should Google THEM, and instantly get more personal information than you'd ever be able to capture in an entire lifetime. A
real-life example? The Bel Air Hotel in LA already Googles first-
time guests upon arrival, based on their reservation details (name
and address), leading to personalized services like assigning guests a
room with morning sun if Googling shows the guest enjoys jogging
early in the day (source: http://blog.outer-court.com).*

So how will this trend affect your business? Consider the example of
the holidaymaker who reviews a hotel, the claimant who reviews the
claim-handling process, or your twinsumer who has found a great
financial adviser. There are literally tens of millions of personal profiles, blogs, and homepages already up and running (whether it's on
Yub, MSN Space, Blogger, TheFaceBook.com, Friendster, FunHi,
Epinions, Hi5, Cyworld, Meetup, Common.net, Tribe.net, or
Cu2.nl). This is "the word of mouse" of the future.

Look at any of these virtual communities and you will realize it's no
longer just about rating books, music, and DVDs. In our fragmented
society, do you still know who is telling your customers to do or buy
what? Are you confident enough in your superior service performance
that you will consistently outdo your competitors' reviews? With our
access to mobile technology, we should expect reviews to become
real-time, entertaining, and even visual. They could potentially make
or break new products or services.

For good or ill, we now longer have "a place" in society. We can dip
in and out of interest groups, find likeminded others, create momentum for our own causes with the click of a button. Look at Yub.com, a
wholly owned subsidiary of Buy.com, which calls itself the world's first
shopping social network. Its mission is to "provide word-of-mouth on
the web, filtered by trusted relationships." Partnering with the likes of
Sony, Apple iTunes, Target, Gap, Linens 'n Things, and Footlocker, its
virtual shopping mall offers 3.3 million products. Yub customers share
their opinions on purchases and everything else in accessible e-profile,
and receive a 1 percent cashback on every item they buy.

The permanent hurry

*I've become convinced that our society now consists of only two
classes of people. It's not a divide by birthright. It's a divide by*

time. There are large numbers of people who spend huge amounts of time to save money and a small group of people who spend huge amounts of money to save time.

(Dr Peter Cochrane, Frontiers)

It's now accepted that many of us are *time poor*. Inside businesses, learning to manage time is at least as important as managing other resources of the enterprise—and per head, often the most expensive training course in the brochure. In our experience, managers at all levels complain about lacking the time to do all they want to do in the day. And if it's bad for those inside organizations, it's just as bad for those outside.

But how has this happened? Why, at the beginning of the twenty-first century, do so many of us complain we have less time than ever before—for work, for our families, to exercise, even to sleep, which we apparently do, on average, for 90 minutes less per night than our parents?

Over the last 20 years the pressures of competition in the market have become manifest in the need to work longer hours. There isn't just the competition between firms, it's the competition between employees too. Furthermore, in the office, there is more and more information to assimilate and more communication to be acknowledged and responded to.

At home, although we have a huge array of labor-saving machines, we do more washing, of clothes and ourselves, than ever before, not to mention the ironing. So the "time saved" seldom adds up to more than 30 minutes a day. Doctors in the United States have coined the term "hurried woman syndrome" to describe juggling a spouse, children, relatives, friends, *and* a boss. In the United Kingdom, physiotherapists say it has become the norm, despite their claim that this hectic lifestyle can put your physical and mental health at risk.

It's not just women. We live in a hurried society. As James Gleick documented in his 1999 book *Faster: The acceleration of just about everything*, we try to speed up even the un-speedable. We obsessively push the "close door" elevator button to give ourselves the illusion we are speeding up the door closure, even though this button—certainly the most worn-out on the panel—does *not* in fact speed up the closing of the door. We try to eliminate meal preparation by eating fast food. A restaurant in Japan has even changed the way we are charged for food; now it simply charges patrons 35 yen per minute!

The result is that a great many people complain about being rushed, overscheduled, stressed, and unable to keep up. We feel

61

frantic, impatient, short-tempered, and frustrated much of the time. What does this mean for your customers and for the people who look after them? It hardly sounds like the conditions needed to mark the start of a beautiful friendship.

The trust implosion

There is a paradox that the more sophisticated media management, public relations and advertising become, the less they appear to work. Part of the problem is that the more power and influence spin doctors and marketing people acquire, the more they themselves become the story. Trust today is a scarce resource. To greater or lesser degrees we distrust the media, the government, and big business. In the UK's recent government elections, parties arguably expended more effort in persuading the electorate to vote at all.

A recent poll (Harris Poll, March 2005) measured the trust US citizens have in important institutions, and compared the results with those in a virtually identical European survey. For many institutions the levels of trust, or distrust, on both sides of the Atlantic were similar. There were also striking differences. US citizens showed much less trust than Europeans in the media and in the United Nations. On the other hand, US citizens trusted religious institutions more than Europeans. Both US citizens and Europeans had relatively high levels of trust in their police and military but both had very little trust in political parties, their governments, trade unions, and notably big business.

The structural features of the media sector in the United States versus those in Europe, particularly in the United Kingdom, underlie the more cynical US attitudes toward the press, radio, and television. Specifically:

1 62 percent of US citizens did not trust "the press." Europeans were a little more confident of the integrity of the press with 46 percent. Trust in the press was highest in Spain (61 percent) and France (60 percent), and lowest in the United Kingdom (20 percent)—with its own special mass-market tabloid journalism.
2 A modest 43 percent of US citizens were inclined to trust the radio; a larger majority of 62 percent of Europeans did so.
3 A substantial 58 percent majority of US citizens did not trust television; while 54 percent majority of Europeans did trust television. Trust in television was highest in Germany (59 percent)

and the United Kingdom (54 percent) and lowest in Italy (37 percent), where Prime Minister Silvio Berlusconi owns several powerful networks.

Majorities in both the United States and Europe did not trust their politicians or their governments. Forty-nine percent of Europeans trusted the United Nations, while 44 percent of US citizens distrusted the UN. Very large majorities of US citizens (77 percent) and Europeans (again 77 percent) distrusted political parties. Substantial majorities of both US citizens (55 percent) and Europeans (63 percent) distrusted their governments. A substantial majority of US citizens (56 percent) distrusted Congress. A substantial majority of Europeans (57 percent) distrusted their parliaments or elected chambers.

With regard to other institutions, large majorities of between three to one and two to one trusted the police and the military in both the United States and in Europe. Large majorities also trust charitable and voluntary organizations. On the other hand, very large majorities in both the United States (70 percent) and in Europe (60 percent) distrust big companies. Respondents also tended not to trust trade unions in both the United States (51 percent) and Europe (50 percent).

But why don't we trust anyone any more? Could it be the fact that big business raided the pension funds and got away with it? What about the weapons of mass destruction that never were? The pedophile scandals of the Catholic Church or the CIA training camps in Afghanistan? And yes, the Red Cross really did use blood infected with HIV and hepatitis to treat Canada's hemophiliacs. With the decline in trust comes a perhaps almost refreshing growth in cynicism. One is reminded of the Hollywood comic actor Jack Black, who commented, "We're in the Dark Ages if it can be the case that J-Lo can have a singing career because of her ass. And let's face it, that's it."

Is there anyone left we can trust? Eighty-eight percent of people are more likely to trust their dads than anyone else when it comes to financial advice on topics such as mortgages, pensions, and investments, and are happy with the advice they have received. This is 10 percent higher that those who were happy with the advice they received from an independent financial adviser (B&CE Benefit Schemes, 2002). In a world where we feel cynical and distrustful our family and friends (real or virtual) are perhaps the most reliable sources of information—and recommendation.

Ethic-quette

In times of social transformation, traditional values often make a comeback. The resurrection of respect and "basic values" in the United Kingdom is an example, and the process is already well underway in the United States, with a surge of morals and values that are often labeled Republican territory, although the political correctness of the left may be a manifestation of the same urge.

There is also, of course, the growth of organic food, "Fairtrade" products, dolphin-friendly tuna, and the whole green movement in general, with its wide-ranging effects on consumer preferences. These days it's commonplace to hear customers asking, "Are those eggs free range?" Or "Was that garment made with child labor?" But how does the ethical dimension work for services?

In many service businesses there is a great deal of concern about retaining staff, since staff retention is often taken as a measure of staff motivation. The degree to which staff are motivated to take care of customers is an important strategic consideration since, other factors being equal, customer loyalty depends on highly skilled service providers who want to impress. The degree to which service organizations become recognizable for their ethical treatment of staff and customers will become increasingly important.

Perhaps the best example is the unease which many customers feel with regard to offshoring services. In the 2004 report "Finding the balance: the effect of offshore customer contact on profit and brand," Contact-Babel, a research and analysis firm in the United Kingdom, found that a significant number of UK customers are reacting negatively to offshore call centers. According to the findings of the research conducted with more than 1000 British adults—who had had personal experience of an offshore contact center—74 percent of UK customers feel more negatively towards the company providing it than they did before.

In the United Kingdom a typical high street bank will save an estimated £9.26 million per year in operating costs by replacing 1000 UK agents with the same number in India. However, if only an extra 0.343 percent of customers defect in protest at this, the bank's revenues will be reduced by the same amount. In 2003, 1.09 per cent of UK banking customers changed banks as a direct result of customer service offshoring.

Customers who have experienced offshore customer contact are four and a half times more likely to have changed their supplier than customers who have had no direct experience of offshoring. Plus, 42 percent of customers said they are less interested in sales calls when they come from outside the country. In the United Kingdom, tele-coms and insurance companies experienced the greatest levels of offshore-related customer defection.

The report suggests the reasons for defection are that customers feel too many companies are using offshore contact centers in an unimaginative and cost-obsessed way which is alienating. Most of the UK public are not against the concept of offshoring, and are prepared to give it a try. However, the experience has often been disappointing and has led to considerable numbers of customers defecting to UK-based competitors, which has made a definite and growing dent in profits—exactly the opposite to what these companies are trying to achieve through offshoring,

One wonders to a degree to which it is the ethical backlash—that customers feel offshoring leads to job losses in the home country or exploitation in the offshore location—or actual customer experience that is behind these statistics of customer defection. Our own research has shown that offshore contact centers certainly do have a role to play in providing service to UK customers. Offshore contact centers can greatly help in improving the quality of service offered. By offering the flexibility of a highly qualified and cost-effective labor pool, the offshore call center industry can help to solve issues that the domestic industry has, such as finding staff for evening and weekend working, providing technical support, replying promptly to e-mails, reducing queuing times, and increasing the service hours that a company can offer to its customers.

There persists, however an ethical dimension, perhaps best illustrated by example. When John Varney, chief technical officer at the British Broadcasting Corporation (BBC) in London, recently signed off a massive, ten-year IT outsourcing deal worth nearly $3.3 billion with Germany's Siemens, he raised the welcome prospect of saving the pioneering UK public broadcaster $50 million a year. In an interesting development, the BBC plans to outsource its IT department. But it will not allow offshoring of the same. Varney said that while off-shoring application development will be permitted, everything else must stay within the United Kingdom. All services, help desks, and network support will be inside the United Kingdom:

The BBC is part of the UK's cultural heritage. It is important that services be delivered from inside the UK and the future of the 1400 staff must be assured.

Rude rage

Good manners help us get on together. It may be that the nineteenth century was a more polite age because life was then more desperate and difficult and politeness was needed to prevent frustration, anxiety, and desperation continually spilling out into violence. Politeness puts others at their ease by smoothing interaction in new situations through abiding by established rules: saying please and thank you, not keeping people waiting, taking turns in conversations, and showing respect for others' feelings and status.

Yet surveys showing widespread perception of a decline in respect and increase in reprehensible behavior in people other than those responding to the survey appear all the time. In 2003, for example, a record number of Germans—164 848—were booked for insulting each other as opposed to fewer than 80 000 in 1990. The gestures are carefully defined in a catalog kept by public prosecutors and include: tapping the forehead with an index finger, which relays the message "you're crazy," forming an "O" with the index finger and thumb to signify a part of the anatomy, and US-inspired use of the middle finger. Verbal insults listed by prosecutors include "stupid cow," "pig-dog" and "riff-raff."

In a survey by Public Agenda, a New York based non-profit organization, 79 percent of US citizens think that rude behavior is a serious problem and 61 per cent of them think it is on the increase. Ninety percent of them also believe rudeness leads directly to violence—which is certainly plausible, since being treated rudely leaves us feeling angry and enraged. You have only to think of what happens on the road, in the air, and even with supermarket trolleys as examples. It's not a problem just in the West—apparently the Chinese government has banned 50 rude phrases from use by service providers in hotels, airports, and shops. That is not a bad idea.

But what evidence is there that rudeness is really on the rise? There is a rumor that directory enquiry services have stopped using the word "please" in order to save time. A quick survey of UK Directory Services found only half the agents appeared to be familiar with this term—and only one offered a "thank you for calling us" message that reminded callers with whom they'd actually been dealing.

While its not clear whether the language we choose to use today is any more salty or shocking than it was in the past, Sam Hill in his 2002 book *60 Trends in 60 Minutes* makes an interesting point:

The case for decline and fall of etiquette is not so clear cut. Were we shipped back in time to the 1920s we would be appalled at the number of horrifying and patronizing attitudes towards and terms for social and ethnic groups that would be sprinkled throughout the conversation.

He argues that in fact we're getting more polite in some ways and less polite in others. Consider the insurance agent who works on the claim line. This agent listens to reports of accidents, losses, and burglaries all day, every day. By the strange priorities of a typical IT system, the information customers must give first is their "policy number" rather than their name. As a result of this system quirk and the alienating nature of the work, many agents actually have to be prompted by the same system just to acknowledge the human being at the end of the phone with "I'm sorry to hear that" before the requisite "Policy number?" Is that rude? We think it is. There is always time to respond to customers' feelings.

Of course, what we consider rude varies from individual to individual—a bit. Someone making small talk when we're in a hurry? Infuriating. Someone trying to rush us when we need time to think? Exasperating. Is it an impossible challenge for service providers?

It may be that differences in individuals' social skills means that someone, somewhere, will always feel he or she is being treated rudely. Rudeness will always be with us, and finger-wagging about polite behavior may seem futile. The implications, however, for businesses wishing to impress customers with their service are serious. Although there is as yet no proof that rudeness is increasing in absolute terms, the significance of the poor impression it creates is bound to increase—especially with our ageing population. Good manners are already perceived to be in desperately short supply, and this makes them a competitive weapon.

Stressfulness of choice

With 11 pieces of clothing there are 39,916,800 ways of getting dressed. Trying one method every minute would take 76 years of life.
(Dr Edward de Bono)

Materially in the West, we've never had it so good. Yet research findings show us that despite the growth in material wealth, we aren't getting any happier. Of course, money does matter—people in rich countries are happier than people in poor countries, but the difference is not as dramatic as one might expect. Once a society's level of per capita wealth takes its people from poverty to adequate subsistence, further increases in income have almost no effect on happiness. There are as many happy people in Poland, for example, as there are in Japan, even though the average Japanese is ten times richer than the average Pole. Comparing happiness between countries is one way of looking at it. A second way is to compare rates of happiness over time. Japan's per capita wealth has increased by a factor of five in the last 40 years, though with no measurable increase in the level of individual happiness.

Why should this be so? Surely a measure of our material well-being must be the ever expanding choices that we now have as a matter of course in almost every category of product, of service, of entertainment, or even of lifestyle. In fact, freedom of choice is something that we take as a mark of our civilization. While no choice is a recipe for human misery, Barry Schwartz in his 2004 book *The Paradox of Choice* has described how the relentless proliferation of choice can also make us feel stressed and even depressed.

A recent study entitled "When Choice is Demotivating" was set up in a food store where customers were accustomed to trying out new products. Researchers set up a table featuring a range of high-quality jams and encouraged customers to taste them—giving each taster a coupon he or she could use for money off if he or she then purchased a jar. In one version of the study, six varieties of the jam were available for tasting; in a second version of the study 24 varieties were available. In either case all 24 varieties were for sale.

There were some fascinating results. The larger array of jams attracted more tasters than the small array, though in both cases the average number of jams tasted was the same. When it came to buying, though, 30 percent of customers exposed to the small array bought a jar of jam, while only 3 percent of those exposed to the large array did so.

The authors of the study speculated about the significance of these results. It appeared that a large array of options may discourage a decision to purchase because the effort to make that decision is significantly increased—so consumers *decide not to decide*. In other studies it has also been found that among consumers who do purchase, the effort of the decision can detract from the results. When people have dismissed many options, it may decrease the satisfaction they experience from what they have actually chosen, because dismissed options may still carry significant attractive benefits. Every choice we make has opportunity costs which can cause us regret.

The number of options can influence our capacity to make decisions, but why does this cause us stress? What matters most of the time is how we feel about the decisions we make. When economists theorize about satisfaction and preference, they assume people seek to maximize their preferences or their satisfaction. They do, but subjective factors are likely to be as important as objective factors here. For example, getting the best objective result—such as the cheapest car insurance—may not be worth much if we feel distrustful of the company or worried that there may be some hidden clause that will compromise us should there be an accident. If we don't feel good about our decisions, we will keep shopping around.

One of the reasons we don't always feel good about choices is the concept of regret. Any time we make a decision and it doesn't turn out well—or we find out about an alternative that would have turned out better—the chances are we will feel regret. Often this is post-decision regret—or buyer's remorse—when we have experienced the unpleasant or unwelcome consequences of a decision we have already made, but sometimes we also anticipate regret.

When we anticipate regret we're asking ourselves, "How will I feel if I buy this insurance now, from this company, when there might be a better deal around the corner?" It raises our emotional stakes in the decision-making process. We would need to feel mighty confident that there would be no such notional deal if we wanted to avoid anticipated regret.

In summary, while we're not saying reduced choice is necessarily good, we are pointing out that the proliferation of choice has presented customers with problems that being loyal to an organization could solve. Schwartz describes the future as a bleak scenario in which after years of economic development and prosperity we will revert back to the time-consuming foraging behavior of our ancestors in which we have to sift for ourselves through more and more options in almost every aspect of life. If this is the way people are to live their lives, loyalty makes a lot of sense.

Authenticity addiction

The changes in the economy over the last four decades have marked a distinct break with the past. The massive shifts that originated in the social and economic conditions following the Second World War have been accelerating in recent years. The arrival of the new knowledge-based economy, the Internet, and e-commerce have changed the pace of customers' demand for service, but not the attributes.

It is certainly the case that previous generations of customers were more easily retained by organizations, though this is not customer loyalty by our definition. Many customers would have been constrained by a lack of choice or need for convenience which no longer apply today. Given the erosion from these types of constraint, there is some evidence that customers are looking for more in the way they live their lives and even the relationships they form with service businesses.

This trend has been heralded amongst sociologists, ecologists, and even advertising companies as a search and need for authenticity, where it defines integrity and trustworthiness. Customers influenced by this trend are easily recognizable—they want to know where their food comes from and what is in it; they want politicians to be more transparent about what they are saying; they want musicians to play rather than mime; they want to speak to a person rather than a machine when they call a helpline.

The desire for authenticity in services is partly an outcome of another one of the trends we have discussed here—the trust implosion. Customers today are much less likely to believe marketing messages than ever before. They want to *experience* the promises service organizations make. Without experience of "a caring attitude" or "helpfulness," the credibility of such claims on the part of an organization are meaningless and easily dismissed.

As life experience teaches us, it's the source of information that we use when judging credibility—and the experience of other consumers, or better still, people we know, that will lend certain businesses this credibility in their service claims, while others will suffer. Clearly, credibility is also deeply rooted in the performance of an organization's charismatic and skilled service providers and the way in which service is provided. For example, treating customers as individual people rather than interchangeable members of a target segment can transform a mundane commercial encounter into a worthwhile, authentic experience. By personal experience or by association, customers find authenticity attractive because authenticity signifies, in every sense, superior quality.

Summary

We have covered seven trends which we have identified among the customers we have been talking to over the last few years. If you want to identify some relevant social trends yourself, it's quite simple. Keep your eyes and ears wide open—seriously. Despite all the hype, most companies don't spend much time talking to customers. If you do, you'll find customers who feel frantically short of time. You can save them time by making sure they never feel the need to shop around. There will be customers who worry about whether to trust you to take care of them, and those looking to be steered through a bewildering set of choices. Others will want to be treated with authentic respect and courtesy.

We believe these trends reveal opportunities for service businesses to dramatically improve the quality of the relationships they have with customers. By understanding the influences in customers' lives, service businesses can serve customers better. Plus, if you impress customers, there is good money to be made.

And the really big money? Well, this doesn't come from following trends. Since loyalty takes time to build, the best opportunity comes from people with original ideas and service propositions who can create trends. We think social conditions are now absolutely ripe for the next trend to be created. This will be the trend among customers to stop shopping around and instead to return to being loyal to a small set of unquestioningly preferred suppliers. How that can be achieved is the subject of the remainder of this book.

4 The benefits of winning customer loyalty

Do customers want to be loyal?

In the 2002 movie *Minority Report*, starring Tom Cruise and directed by Steven Spielberg, there is a scene that should excite the interest of anyone with a professional interest in customer loyalty. Set in the year 2054, the movie depicts a fairly benevolent society where everyone is identifiable by personal retina scanning.

In one scene that is designed, for plot reasons, to illustrate how readily the outlawed Cruise can be identified by his eyeballs, the actor strides rapidly though a shopping mall, where he is incessantly bombarded by personalized messages spoken by loudspeakers fitted into advertising hoardings he passes. These messages offer him all sorts of products tailored to his precise needs. The relentless bombardment of the messages suggests by implication that in the year 2054, the idea that someone might voluntarily want to be loyal to a particular supplier is a nonsense.

What about the situation now, in the first decade of the twenty-first century rather than the sixth?

While we must be careful in making observations about which received wisdoms dominate in the business world—for prevailing attitudes in the business world are notoriously difficult to pin down—few would deny that more and more organizations are despairing of being able to win loyalty from customers. The rapidly increasing use of remote service dispensed by contact centers, the ever more important role of the Internet in commerce (in which disloyalty is supposed to be only the click of a mouse away), plus the general sense that our fast-moving, highly mobile society does not encourage a climate of loyalty, all conspire to support the notion that most likely customers want to be *dis*loyal.

But we very firmly believe that they don't. The truth of the matter, we believe, is that people want to belong nowadays *more than they ever have*, especially because the plethora of choice facing customers today can, as we saw in the previous chapter, be highly stressful. People want to belong: to their loved ones, to their friends, to familiar communities (witness the enormous popularity of soap operas featuring fictional tight-knit communities). Above all, as far as this book is concerned, we believe people want to belong to the community of customers of organizations they know, trust, and like.

It is possible to witness a real-life example of how the product focus dominates in the fermenting pressure of developing economic systems without the need for a time machine. Simply look to the East. The burgeoning economic growth in China offers some interesting parallels. Certainly the retail banking industry in China is in its infancy compared with that in Britain and the United States. Yet China has been changing fast. Previously under socialism, there was only one bank (the "People's Bank," inevitably). There is now a market economy with four large banks. In the beginning, each bank had a different business speciality, but now they all cover everything, so there is genuine competition between them, and smaller banks are entering the market too. So the question how to keep customers is arising. But, unlike in Britain and the West generally, this question has *only just* arisen and the main focus is for the time being on getting products right—"offering the right competitive products in the long term."

In the past, the private sector could hardly borrow from the banks, so firms all looked after their own finances, but now such borrowing has started. Given how much is still to be privatized, the challenge for Chinese banks is to get lending rights to the companies that are about to join the private sector.

Also, ten years ago there were hardly any personal loans or mortgages, but they are just starting now, and Bank of China offers them. They are set to grow considerably. In terms of social trends however, the Chinese aren't used to borrowing: only 5 percent have current accounts, and very few have credit cards—everything is cash. So the potential for growth is obvious. But the Chinese do save—45 percent of their income, on average, as opposed to 4 percent in the UK. The insurance market is just starting to develop.

Yet customer loyalty, even in this massive market, must include the service as well as the product ethic. Since 1992 the ten-times winner of *Euromoney* magazine's Best Bank in China award has been the Bank of China. The bank has also been included in the Fortune Global 500 for 13 consecutive years. Significantly, as Mr Li of the

Bank of China points out, "as well as attracting new clients, the Bank has to serve its existing customers too, as this is clearly the best way of marketing."

Further evidence supporting this point is that in many industrial and commercial sectors, there is a clear correlation between the level of loyalty an organization manages to attain and its profitability. James Dyson's revolutionary bagless vacuum cleaner, for example, has made him a billionaire and won millions of customers around the world who are fiercely loyal to the product which comes bundled up with so much service that it is not unreasonable to describe it as a service brand. The late Sidney de Haan's organization Saga—which started out as a holiday company and then diversified very successfully into financial services—is a superb example of an organization that has consistently and regularly won an abundance of loyalty from its customers.

To conclude; there really seems little doubt at all that customers want to be loyal. The message to organizations must be: accept this point and integrate it intimately into the fabric of your business strategy, and see your sales and profits climb.

The crucial importance of the lifetime value of a customer

The lifetime value of a loyal customer (the value of a loyal customer to an organization during the customer's economically active life) can be enormous. Researchers at Harvard Business School have estimated that the lifetime revenue stream from a loyal pizza eater can be $8000, a car purchaser US$332 000, and a purchaser of commercial aircraft literally billions.

The problem, though, is that most businesses find it very difficult to think in terms of financial consequences of a customer relationship beyond the current deal, or perhaps the current budget period. A piece of equipment, a product development, or a brand may have long-term value, but customer relationships exist only in the present. The startling fact is that loyal customers actually become more valuable over time.

All of us know that attracting new customers costs. Indeed for many businesses, the profits gained from the initial deal or even during the first year may not defray the costs of gaining the customer in the first place. Real value only starts to develop when the customer is able to purchase a variety of products or services from you and savings are gained through aligning processes and preferred supplier relationships. So if the customer is loyal, and is retained because the quality of your service inspires the customer to remain loyal to you, the customer should become increasingly profitable, because it should be possible to reduce the cost of selling to the customer and reduce to zero—after the first year—the cost of acquiring the customer. In the meantime, the customer may well be likely to spend more money with you every year.

TeleCheck International, a check acceptance company, calculated the lifetime value of a customer by factoring in increased revenues from its base product, declining per-unit service costs (from customer and supplier learning effects), and increased sales from purchases of a new product, and estimated profits from referrals by a satisfied customer. Telecheck's management estimated that a 20 percent annual increase in revenue from its base product could produce a 33 percent annual increase in operating profit from the customer relationship. The total five-year stream of operating profit—£52 000—was used to justify £4 000 spent on acquiring the customer in the first year.

More about the commercial benefits of offering customer loyalty

Today's business world is full of examples of organizations that provide merely middling or poor levels of customer service, but which still continue in business and even to thrive. This being so, what *precise* link can identify between customer loyalty and the commercial benefits accruing to the organization that wins it?

It's true that many organizations do indeed find that they can keep on ticking over and making a reasonable profit by delivering only an ordinary level of customer service and winning ordinary levels of customer loyalty. Any organization operating in a large retail market such as the United Kingdom and United States is likely to find that many customers come to it as a consequence of the sheer fact that there are so many customers out there who will be looking for what the organization can offer.

But winning customers in this way can hardly be satisfactory for an organization that wants to maximize its profitability and success during difficult competitive times. Delivering a mediocre or only ordinary level of customer service cannot, logically, be the best way to do business. Indeed, one might reasonably ask why any organization deserves to be in business at all, if delivering a mediocre or only ordinary level of service is the best it can do.

Besides, there is the clearest evidence that, in fact, organizations that do set out on a crusade to offer *great* rather than merely good customer service can expect to win major commercial advantages.

Let's start by looking at the cost argument.

Great customer service and cost

Does offering great customer service really make sense from a cost perspective? There has often been a perception on the part of organizations that the cost of delivering great customer service cannot really be justified; that great customer service and profitability are, in effect, mutually exclusive.

True, few organizations would deny the strategic benefits of making every effort to maximize the quality of customer service. Organizations accept that these benefits would typically include increased customer retention and much better staff motivation—resulting in improved retention of quality staff. But are there also likely to be clear cost benefits for an organization in putting a major emphasis on improving its customer service?

Strangely enough, attempts to analyze the cost advantages to an organization of improving the quality of its customer service are surprisingly thin on the ground. New research and field work we have carried out at Cape Consulting suggests that the cost benefit issue relating to customer service should ideally be considered from three perspectives. Taken together, and with illustrative examples, they add up to a reliable and solid justification that investing in improving the quality of service offered to customers is not only the most potent of strategic initiatives, but also has the clearest possible cost justification attached to it.

Cutting the costs of poor service

First, let's look at the cost benefits likely to be gained from cutting the costs of poor service.

Every organization which is in business will incur costs associated with providing service to its customers. In many industries these customer-servicing costs are a substantial proportion of total costs.

What is true of customer service generally is particularly true of customer service as delivered through contact centers. These were introduced to save money, but are in reality still a major cost, especially for large organizations.

In practice, there is clear evidence to indicate that about 10 percent of the time in business-to-business markets—and at least 20 percent of the time in consumer markets—customers who deal with a call center still wind up with a query, a concern, or an unmet need after their first interaction with the contact center, which will prompt them to contact the center again. These instances of renewed contact in practice cost organizations running contact centers substantial sums. The instances of renewed contact are often known within the customer service arena as "failure demand."

Research has also shown that even after a second attempt at resolution, about 5 percent of the group of consumers who felt they needed the second attempt at resolution may, in fact, still need further help to get their needs addressed. This costly, and all too common, scenario is known as "escalation."

One of the paradoxes of the contact center industry is therefore that contact centers actually create additional work that is only necessary because the inherent nature of a contact center can create a need for additional interaction with customers. It is a curious example in business of a powerful resource creating additional work that might not otherwise have been necessary.

The fact that the problem of failure demand is especially acute in the consumer industry is really a momentous revelation, and one that organizations would be irresponsible to ignore, especially since all the evidence available suggests that failure demand is an equally serious problem across all consumer sectors.

It follows that a contact center must, as far as possible, take every step to maximize the likelihood that customers will be happy with the first contact (or one might even call it the "primary contact") they have with the center.

Ensuring that contact center agents know the correct behaviors on their part that will maximize the likelihood that the query will be handled correctly first time round, and ensuring that agents know how to put these behaviors into practice are absolutely essential if wasted costs are to be avoided. Again, this brings us to the notion of the loyalty-building experiences (LBEs) that are such an integral part of delivering top levels of customer loyalty, and are discussed in detail elsewhere in this book.

One of our clients recently drew the conclusion that for every one percent of improvement in the quality of the customer service experience, at least four percent of servicing costs could be saved. In any customer service operation involving large numbers of customers being looked after every day by a contact center, the potential cost savings of "getting it right" can be enormous.

An additional crucial point that needs making here is that cost-savings achieved by organizations, working with their contact center agents to modify and improve the behaviors these agents display to customers, do not need to involve any capital costs. However, this idyllic state of being will in practice only be achieved if loyalty-building experiences are in place and are being pursued seriously by contact center agents. The following worked example shows precise details of cost savings achievable by improving the quality of service provided in contact centers.

Quantifying the potential savings can engage management and galvanize action as it represents the direct link between investment in service excellence and the bottom line. By improving the customer's first contact, an organization can avoid the costs associated with escalation—as well as knowing that loyalty and retention are also being positively impacted.

Worked example 1

More and more organizations are relying on call centers to provide the "customer service" function. This simple example shows how a reduction in repeat calls (failure demand) can not only improve customer feeling toward the organization but also save the company money. This is in fact a real-life example of a call center with which we recently worked. The same principles will tend to apply in any customer interaction.

This worked example is based on the case of a 250-seat call center taking 200 000 inbound calls per month. This example assumes that the call center achieves a first-time resolution in 70 percent of calls. Second-time resolution is achieved in 25 percent of calls, and the remaining 5 percent of interactions entail three or more contacts.

Although these figures may not be accurate in your organization they help illustrate the point. The figures are certainly realistic. Why? Because when customers have to make more than one phone call to achieve resolution of an issue, the following all increase:

- the time taken by the call center agent to read customer details
- the time taken to resolve the query
- the time taken to reassure the customer that he or she will be satisfied this time
- the escalation to supervisor/manager level and complaints handling.

Now let's look at some sample arithmetic of the figures in this example:

Number of inbound calls per month	= 200 000
Cost of a service interaction at first call	= £2
Cost of a service interaction at second call	= £4
Cost of escalated contact (three or more contacts)	= £10

Total cost of service in the call center:

70 percent of 200 000 (140 000) x £2	= £280 000
25 percent of 200 000 (50 000)x £4	= £200 000
5 percent of 200 000 (10 000) x £10	= £100 000
Total monthly cost of service	= £580 000

Based on these figures, by reducing the number of customers having to call twice to resolve a matter by just 5 percent, an organization would create significant cost improvements, as follows:

75 percent of 200 000 (150 000) x £2	= £300 000
20 percent of 200 000 (40 000) x £4	= £160 000
5 percent of 200 000 (10 000) x £10	= £100 000
Total monthly cost of service	= £560 000

This will lead to a saving of £20 000 per month in cost of contact alone. In the longer term this will lead to dramatic savings from a reduction in number of calls overall, a reduction in number of calls escalating beyond two calls, and—generally—much less "fire-fighting." The result will therefore be more opportunities to sell, plus engendering a more positive feeling towards the organization, and all the good things that will bring.

Increased revenues deriving from impressing customers

The second aspect of the cost benefit involves increasing revenues by impressing customers.

Other things being equal, customers want to show loyalty to an organization. Quite apart from anything else, it is easier for a customer to stick with one particular supplier once a suitable one has been found. Organizations that are aware of this practical element in customers' behavior can benefit from giving customers additional reasons to be loyal.

In practice, the evidence that making a successful effort to impress customers is likely to lead to the winning of additional revenue is conclusive. Specifically, good service should result in:

- *More repeat business:* creating 20–40 percent lower selling costs.
- *Longer customer retention:* up to 50 percent longer.
- *More referrals:* creating 20–40 percent lower promotion costs.

Worked example 2

Let's now look at the specific financial implications of the above figures. The figures we use here are likely to be typical of a medium-sized contact center.

Number of transactions per month	200 000
From a reliable sample, service incidences which are judged as "satisfactory,"	70 percent
versus those judged as "excellent," and generating recommendation	20 percent
Annual profits per customer	£100

In this example, with 20 percent of the 200 000 contacts being deemed worthy of recommendation, we are talking about 40 000 customers altogether who make recommendations. Modern research into customer loyalty suggests that when people do recommend a vendor, they are likely to recommend to up to a total of eight other people.

Using these figures, we might expect that in the best-case scenario, the 40 000 incidences worthy of recommendation do in fact result in a total of 320 000 actual recommendations. It is difficult to be dogmatic about the relationship between number of recommendations and number of new customers won. However, our experience at Cape Consulting leads us to believe that an average figure of one new customer being won for every 50 recommendations is reasonably workable and accurate.

Consequently, for the 320 000 recommendations here, we might expect the organization to win 6400 new customers. Assuming that annual profit is £100 per customer—which is a reasonable assumption for a large consumer organization—this equates to a gain in profit of £640 000 annually.

Again, this improvement can be achieved without capital cost.

The impact on the brand

Third, it is essential to bear in mind that improved customer service can have a major and long-lasting positive impact on the value of your brand. Since we are talking here principally about customer loyalty stemming from exceptionally good service, we are correspondingly talking principally about service brands.

Since the 1980s there has been a dramatic increase in the extent to which the economic significance of brands—both product brands and service brands—has been recognized. Furthermore—and this point is in our view rarely given the attention it deserves—more and more *product* brands now contain strong elements of customer service.

In practice, many organizations have created brands that embody a significant amount of service, yet the organizations do not pay anything like as much attention as they should to the actual service experience that goes along with these brands. The experiences that customers have during their encounter with the company's service representative can significantly enhance or damage the brand.

In practice, there are significant challenges in translating a brand's values into a set of behaviors that can be delivered by the people who work in customer-facing roles. A key component of success is getting the service climate right. This service climate is created through the visioning, leadership, and management of the environment where service can thrive. To make the change to the service climate truly effective and enduring, an organization must be brave enough to challenge the way work has been done in the past.

We look in greater deal at the impact of improved customer service on the commercial impact and value of the brand in the next chapter, which focuses on customer loyalty and branding.

Overall, what lessons can we learn from everything above? Perhaps the two most important lessons are:

1. An organization must be careful to avoid implementing a performance management system that disproportionately rewards staff for their productivity as far as dealing with customers is concerned, rather than their expertise and emotional devotion to giving their customers a great experience.
2. The organization must develop ways to measure staff performance by embodying measures of the quality of the experience the member of staff gives to customers and the referrals generated by the customers with whom that member of staff has interacted.

The cost argument—a conclusion

In general, organizations have always tended to regard good customer service as being "nice to have," but have many times suspected there to be a dichotomy between achieving good customer service and achieving key financial goals. In other words, many organizations have in the past regarded the delivery of good customer service as being a luxury they could not necessarily afford: they have believed that first-rate customer service and profitability may be mutually exclusive.

Our work at Cape Consulting, however, indicates that this is not at all the case. In fact, far from being mutually exclusive, top-notch customer service and profitability go hand-in-hand. Above all, these figures indicate that it is much more sensible to regard great customer service less as a cost than as an investment, and one likely to give a faster—and greater—payback than many organizations might have expected.

Delivering on the customer service promise

So the cost argument in favor of offering great customer service reigns supreme. But there is unquestionably also a powerful, solid, strategic sheer commercial reason in favor of an organization offering its consumer customers great service.

When a business offers a brand to its customers it extends them a promise that should be exciting, memorable—and, most importantly, deliverable. Keep your promise, and you can have every expectation your customers will be delighted to commit themselves to you for as long as you continue to deliver.

The promise consists of the benefits the customers can expect the brand to bring them. The brand's advertising and marketing will enlarge on this promise, but the only dynamic that will *deliver* the promise will be the customer's *real experience* of the brand. Key factors will be the brand's quality, consistency, and the value for money customers perceive the brand as offering.

For many brands, the quality of the associated customer service will play a major role in delivering the brand's promise. In fast-moving consumer goods (fmcg) markets the role of the customer service element in the brand is hardly significant. A chocolate bar, for example, does not come bundled up with any customer service, though a box of washing powder might do, if there is a helpline number or a website address on the box. But in complex service offerings—areas such as financial services, hospitality, the motor industry, professional services, and most areas of retail—the quality of the customer experience is a vital element, indeed probably the decisive element of delivering on the brand's promise.

A crucially important question

The crucial question to ask yourself is: does the level of the customer experience you offer play a significant role in winning you competitive differentiation? If it does, then as a matter of sheer logic and commonsense, you need to focus on taking every step to maximize the quality of the customer experience you deliver with your brand.

Many organizations, aware of the importance of customer service, try to "up the ante" by launching specific initiatives focusing on customer service. But experience suggests, and a knowledge of human psychology tends to confirm, that such initiatives are not likely to be effective.

By definition, initiatives are conceived as separate, self-contained projects. Such projects tend to be vulnerable to indifference, inertia, and to being discarded if trading conditions worsen. Also, your staff may detect that the initiative is essentially a fad and not something they need to take too seriously.

Even the idea of an organization having a customer service department might imply that the organization thinks it can hive off the responsibility for serving the customer to a specialized department in the same way that it can delegate responsibility for functions such as transport, catering, human resources, and so on. The organization might be tempted to believe it can solve its customer service challenge by adopting this "silo" mentality and approach.

What really needs to happen is that all of the organization's departments must assess on a continuous basis how they impact on the customer and if necessary they must put changes in place. What must be avoided, above all, are conflicting priorities within departments which jeopardize the objective of consistently delivering superb service.

By all means do let the customer service department manage the customer service operations, but don't allow yourself to fall into the trap of thinking that all the responsibility for delivering a competitively differentiated customer experience can be diverted to the customer service department.

Why the holistic view is key

Instead, you need to take a much more holistic view, and strive to ensure that everyone at the organization, and every functional department, are all working together in unison to deliver the same caliber and quality of service—in effect a seamless service—just like every drop of wine in a bottle contributes to the overall experience of its flavor.

Adopting this approach to customer service is not just an altruistic act on the part of the organization; there is a significant body of research that shows conclusively a close correlation between "truly impressed" customers and profitability.

Why merely "satisfying" customers is not enough

Note the use of the term "truly impressed." All the evidence suggests that organizations cannot confidently expect much commercial edge, or indeed any at all, from customers they merely satisfy. An organization looking to win long-term loyalty and trust from a customer is in an analogous position to a suitor wooing a prospective lover. Would your highest romantic aspiration be to marry someone with whom you are merely "satisfied"? Hardly. So why would you expect your customers to feel differently when they consider whether to enter into a "marriage" with an organization's brand?

Chapter 6 of this book looks in more detail at the nature of this need for customers to be truly impressed by the quality of service being offered by an organization.

The two crucial requirements

Today, there are two major dimensions to the challenge of delivering a customer service experience that consistently impresses and so differentiates a business.

First, the organization's board and senior management team need to see the customer service experience as the core of an organization's being, and central to its business strategy, not merely as an "initiative" or the responsibility of some specialized department. Directors and senior managers must be "onboard" and "on-brand": consistently and *authentically* committed to implementing the organization's customer service strategy. They need to understand the implications of that strategy at a holistic level, and to grasp its fit (or not) with other, perhaps longer-standing, strategies and commitments.

Indeed, any organization that wishes to show that it is taking its customer service really seriously should consider the ultimate test of an organization's commitment to its customers—and to the long-term commercial benefits this commitment brings. This is that the organization's senior executives are ready to link their salaries and bonuses to the positive impact their organization has on the customers' experience.

Second, organizations must have the imagination and sincerity to view customer service principally from the perspective of the customer and the customer's needs rather than purely from the point of view of the organization's own requirements.

The danger of the "CRM" mentality

Proof that many—perhaps most—organizations often don't approach the customer with sincerity at all, and don't view customer service principally from the customer's point of view, is seen in the popularity of Customer Relationship Management (CRM) systems. In many cases, calling the system a Customer Relationship Management system at all is intellectually a trifle dishonest, because these systems tend to be programed not to deliver a *relationship* to the customer but to maximize the opportunity to *sell* to them.

Whatever CRM systems designers claim, technology alone cannot deliver sincerity, authenticity, and genuine respect to customers. Only people can do that. Worst of all, too many CRM systems are delivered as essentially stand-alone technological solutions that aren't intimately integrated with the organization's customer service strategy and its people strategy. CRM solutions are hardly ever deployed holistically. They are, in most cases, simply a technological initiative.

The right approach to managing customer-facing staff

One extremely potent practical measure an organization can take to effecting a radical improvement in its customer services is to introduce "customer-facing" teams trained to deal with, as far as possible, all customer requests. Organizations might baulk at the investment and training necessary to achieve this objective, but in practice the increased customer loyalty, and a reduction in the volume of queries arising from customers who do not feel their needs were properly dealt with first time round, are likely to justify it abundantly.

Other practical steps that really work

What other specific practical steps should organizations take to ensure that they have the best chance of effecting the radical improvement in their approach to customer service that is required, and putting it into practice?

Experience suggests that the following steps are the most important:

1. Analyze where your organization is *now* in terms of excellence in delivering customer service, and where it *wants* to be. In particular, look hard at what you think you are doing in terms of generating—again in an authentic and sincere way—the right feelings in customers, so that you can truly impress them.
2. Directors and senior managers need to start working together, now, with a concerted purpose, to focus the whole organization on making the customer experience central to what the organization does. This activity should above all be directed at understanding the implications for the organization of offering the caliber of customer service it wants to offer. The organization may need to restructure so that it can present itself as customer-centric. The "silo" mentality, where the organization sees customer service as simply something handled by a specialist department that operates in splendid strategic isolation, must be avoided at all costs.
3. Think hard about, and focus intensely on, what have been described as "moments of truth." These are the *particularly*

important touchpoints between your customers and your organization where good service is likely to make an especially strong positive impact on your customers, and conversely where bad service is likely to have an especially destructive or negative effect on the relationship.

Not only should you take every step to ensure that "moments of truth" touchpoints offer your customers really positive experiences, but you need to ensure that the quality of the experience is consistent across *all* touchpoints. A great experience the customer received in, say, a bank branch will be completely squandered if the following day the same customer has a negative experience when talking to one of your call center staff. And don't forget that it is unfortunately the case that people tend to remember bad experiences longer than good ones. (Seven times longer, according to recent research.)

4. At a simple, elemental level: make sure you have staff in place who *genuinely* care about customers. The giant food retail chain Asda has a saying, "recruit for attitude, train for skills." You should in fact recruit, assess, and reward staff as much on their devotion to customers as on factors such as the sales they generate and their productivity.

5. Take what steps are necessary to give all appropriate people at your organization the tools to *measure* the beneficial effects of adopting a comprehensive, organization-wide focus on customers. This may require you to develop tools for measuring, in a balanced way, the different impact various departments have on the customer relationship.

6. Remember you are ultimately seeking to win commercial benefits and financial pay-offs from your efforts to offer customers an authentic experience which *truly impresses* them and encourages them to trust your organization and so win their long-term loyalty. You are ultimately seeking to induce your customers to enter with you into what can—not unreasonably—be described as a commercial marriage. Success in achieving this aim is enormously important nowadays, when winning a new customer is far more difficult and expensive than retaining an existing one.

When you make a decisive, sincere and authentic effort to turn your organization into a holistic, comprehensively focused entity that is passionate about the quality of customer service it offers, you are reinventing—and rediscovering—precisely *why* you are in business in the first place.

Ideally, you want your customers to make a commercial marriage with you, and for the honeymoon to last forever.

Great customer service in the business-to-business world

Talking of honeymoons, why do so few relationships between vendors and customers in the business-to-business worlds remain mutually delightful beyond the honeymoon period?

So far in this chapter we have been focusing on the potential effects of offering great customer service to an organization that is mainly doing business with consumers. But there is also an important argument to consider in relation to organizations that do business with business-to-business customers.

In the world of business books such as this, the importance of the business-to-business world is often de-emphasized, or even forgotten entirely. But in fact the business-to-business side of economies is of course of massive importance. And in fact there are important points to make about the great potential significance of customer service to business-to-business organizations.

In practice, reliable industry research suggests that the way to win and retain business-to-business (B2B) customers in today's highly competitive marketplaces is to give them quality service delivered with passion rather than focus excessively on price.

Other research suggests that B2B organizations can regularly expect to win as much as 50 percent more business from existing customers if they devote themselves to understanding what these customers really want.

Organizations that sell to consumers spend millions of pounds every year finding out what consumers think of their products and services and identifying what will motivate consumers to buy more. B2B organizations, on the other hand, rarely take as much trouble to find out what their customers think of them, even though B2B contracts are often enormously valuable. It seems that B2B suppliers often believe they have an innate and reliable knowledge of what their customers think of them. The evidence, however, suggests that in many cases they don't.

Recent research published by TARP—a consultancy that specializes in measuring customer satisfaction—reveals that regardless of the contract size, around 25 percent of B2B customers in the United Kingdom say they would not complain to their supplier about poor service.

This finding is confirmed by our own research at Cape Consulting. Most business customers we have interviewed say that while they will discuss operational failures with suppliers, they are less comfortable giving feedback about relationship management.

The need to maintain a working relationship prevents them revealing the true strength of their feelings. There is, therefore, a serious danger that the first time a B2B supplier knows that a particular customer is unhappy is after the customer has gone to a competitor.

The "80 percent of business from 20 percent of customers" rule

It's an established fact that in a typical B2B organization, about 80 percent of business comes from about 20 percent of customers. This being so, a B2B supplier runs the risk of losing significant turnover if one of its major customers decides to move to a competitor. So there should be no debate—you should invest time in understanding exactly *why* your major customers buy from you and what you can do further to satisfy them.

Cape Consulting set out to investigate B2B organizations' views on their suppliers. The key finding—that B2B suppliers can increase their revenue from a customer by as much as 50 percent—stems from that research.

All the senior executives we interviewed said that suppliers who delivered what they promised and managed relationships effectively could win "significant" new business from their organization. Only a few valued that additional opportunity at less than 25 percent of what they were currently spending. Our research also found that far from awarding contracts just on price, most organizations are willing to pay a price premium to keep on working with B2B suppliers whom they perceive as really caring about their business.

When a B2B supplier loses a major customer, it frequently makes excuses about the reasons, often persuading itself that the account was only lost because a competitor offered a better financial deal.

Any organization that is tempted to make this assumption should perhaps consider asking itself whether *it* ever moves vital contracts, supplied by excellent organizations with which it has strong, long-term, mutually beneficial relationships, *only on price*. Few organizations can genuinely answer in the affirmative to this. This being so, it is worth the organization asking itself why its customers might do this.

One senior executive of a major UK insurer, discussing this point with us soon after ending a relationship with a major supplier, said:

> *Our supplier will have told themselves they lost the deal on grounds of price, but in fact they made no effort to develop relationships around the company. They started out with all the advantages of brand, product range and being the incumbent relationship. If they had lived up to their original promise we would have happily paid a bit more—but for the sub-standard service we received we might as well save some money and take a risk on someone new.*

How to prevent a business-to-business relationship from going stale

So often it seems that a supplier/customer relationship that starts out with great enthusiasm on both sides simply goes stale. Why does this happen?

Perhaps it is because most people tend to find new relationships and new situations more exciting than existing or "old" ones. The challenge of winning business, the satisfaction of beating competitors is undoubtedly good for the ego. No wonder we pay great attention to making the sale and getting the relationship off the ground.

Whether or not you agree, there's no doubt that a huge amount of time, effort, and personal pride goes into winning a big contract. Suppliers present their best features, like eager suitors on a date. They make commitments about delivery, put their best people on the project, and make it clear they see the deal as a partnership.

Once the contract is won, the customer is pleased to have found the right people for the job; the supplier heaves a sigh of relief and top-team attention turns to where the next big contract is coming from. As the marketing director of one of the country's best known charities told us:

> *It's like a marriage. When they want your business they flirt with you, they offer ideas and excitement, we really believe we are going places together, but once they've won, all the sparkle and enthusiasm wanes and we are left wondering whether we chose the right partner after all.*

The difficulty for most suppliers is that delivering what has been promised demands a different mindset from the heady "romantic" phase of the actual winning of the business, just as a successful long-term marriage demands a different mindset from the early days of dating and courtship.

What the new customer really wants is to feel that it is getting access at all times to the same caliber of people who sold it the service: people who really want to understand the customer's business and can spot opportunities to grow it, people who can bring new ideas to the table—in short people who can add value. And that's how opportunities arise for the supplier to win more business from the customer.

For a supplier, finding out what matters most to its most important business customers is not an add-on; it should be something a supplier does as a matter of course. At Cape Consulting we have found that even the most senior people in a customer organization will willingly give their time to providing feedback if they think it will improve existing relationships and ultimately help them grow their business. Customers genuinely like being asked. Individuals stake their own reputation on the deals they do with you. They need you to deliver; they want the relationship to work.

So what positive steps can you take to develop lasting relationships that will create business opportunities for you and your customers?

- *Never forget—you are the supplier.* "They treat me as though I have a dotted-line responsibility to send them money," a managing director of a financial services company told us recently, explaining why he had decided to put out to tender a sizeable contract that he would have in principle been happy to keep with the incumbent. Corporate arrogance is one of the biggest failings to which suppliers are prone. Big-brand suppliers too often forget that they are just that: suppliers. The value of the contract may be high, but that doesn't automatically turn the supplier relationship into a partnership. Imposing your processes on your customers, changing the account team without telling them, withdrawing agreed services with no negotiation, canceling meetings at short or no notice are all examples of common ways in which suppliers disappoint customers and ultimately let them down.
- *Make sure your customers feel valued*: Remember they bought from you because they liked what you had to offer. They liked the people they met, so make sure the top teams stay in touch. Block out time

in your diary, sit down, and make contact. You may be the most important person in your company—but you are not more important than your customers. There may be occasions when internal issues or other meetings seem more pressing, but keep cancellations to the minimum. Follow up problems personally and make it clear to everyone in your company that existing customers are your best opportunity for business growth. By the way, don't make the mistake of thinking (as many suppliers do) that corporate hospitality is a substitute for a business meeting where the nitty-gritty aspects of your relationship with your customer get attended to and the customer's problems solved. Corporate hospitality is one thing; business meetings something else.

- *Deliver what you promised and keep on delivering it*: B2B relationships are normally based around service agreements so there's really no excuse for failing to deliver the standard you committed to. If operational problems crop up, don't keep quiet and hope your customers won't notice, inform them in good time—then they have a chance to manage the impact of the problem on their reputation and business.

- *Get to know your customer's people*: Even though your B2B relationship may be focused around only a small number of people at your customer's organization, get to know as many people there as you can. There may be other business opportunities around, so ask for introductions. Take the time to meet front-line people, very often they have the best ideas about how service can be improved and you will demonstrate you genuinely want to know how the business works.

- *Make sure your customers are "the first to know"*: Any change in your organization that is going to affect your customers needs to be communicated before the grapevine gets to work. Customers feel valued if you make sure they are kept informed. Remember also that a common complaint from B2B customers is that the people who look after their account change too frequently. Make sure there's a range of contacts in place, so that one or two people moving won't have so much impact. Think through the effect of organizational changes, and if you are convinced the changes will be positive, sell the benefits.

- *Continue to flirt with your customers both new and old*: The secret of keeping your customers happy is to continue paying them attention. "Flirt" with them in a business sense. Don't just concentrate on the day-to-day; make time for "blue sky" conversations; you never know where they might lead. Really get to know your customers' business, find out what they want to achieve, identify where you can help—and say what more you can do. If they don't know what more you have to offer they may start looking around for other suppliers of services you could have supplied.

- *Take the trouble and time to research how your customers think of you*: It's an unfortunate truth that in a B2B situation the way you are treating one customer is likely to be the way you are treating all of them. So find out what your customers think of your organization and the way it does business.
- *Never leave a vacuum*: If you are not a full partner in the relationship, someone else will step in and fill the gap. No matter how long you have been working with a customer, be aware that your competitors will be putting their top people in front of your customer, they'll be making creative proposals and promising an exciting future together, in the same way you did when you really wanted the business.
- *Don't allow the honeymoon to end*: If the relationship works well, your customers won't want to part with you, and they'll invite you do more work for them, not less. This is equally true whether you are in a business-to-consumer or business-to-business sector.
- *Never let the honeymoon end*: that really is the phrase that governs the winning of customer loyalty, no matter where our time machine has taken us.

5 Customer loyalty and service brands

The promise offered by the brand

We saw in the previous chapter that when an organization offers a brand to its customers it is in effect extending a promise to them. What is the nature of this promise? Nothing less than a pledge to improve their lives in some significant way.

Ultimately all brands have certain emotional expectations bound up with them relating to life improvements the customer will expect to obtain from the brand. The expectation may or may not turn out to be justified, but it will certainly be there.

A brand's promise will typically relate to one or more of the following type of benefit the customer is likely to experience as a result of choosing the brand in question. This list is not, however, exclusive:

- financial (e.g. cost-savings or perceived value for money)
- physical gratifications (e.g. taste, warmth, comfort)
- status (e.g. the customer feels more important, more knowledgeable, or of a higher social class as a result of interacting with the brand)
- stimulation (e.g. the customer enjoys a particular artiste's music, or a particular movie, or generally feels more excited as a result of interacting with the brand)
- peace of mind (e.g. a life insurance brand gives customers the gratification of knowing that if they die suddenly their families will be protected)
- health benefits
- sentimental associations (e.g. a mother buys the Marmite brand of yeast extract to put on toast for her children because she used to have it on toast herself when she was a child).

Product brands

The word "brand" derives from an old Germanic word meaning "burnt." Originally a brand was simply a burning or charred log or stick. Later—by the mid-seventeenth century—it came to mean a mark of ownership that was placed (branded) on cattle, horses, and other domesticated animals.

By the early nineteenth century, the word "brand" had also come to mean a particular make or kind of goods that would usually bear a trademark. The obvious purpose of this kind of brand was to distinguish one particular commercial offering from another. The brand was a type of badge showing in effect the originator of the product in question.

Gradually, as the notion of the brand evolved and gathered popularity, it came to be associated with a particular set of benefits. As we have seen, brands became extremely important in nineteenth-century commerce, because they allowed one particular offering to be distinguished from another. In particular they provided a simple commercial mechanism for suppliers who were prepared to invest a great deal in the quality of their branded product.

Product brands are in a highly enviable position as far as customer loyalty is concerned. As product brands are, by definition, tangible objects, how they are perceived by consumers is totally within the control of the supplying organization. The discipline of marketing was developed against this product-based scenario: where the marketing department is responsible for understanding customers' expectations and for managing the delivery of the company's offer to its customers. In effect, the relationship a company has with its customers is marketing-led and is governed by the "4 Ps of marketing", namely:

- product specification
- price
- place (or distribution)
- promotion.

By varying one or more of these variables, a company can successfully position its product brand to deliver its promise to customers. And, because the financial rewards of successful brands can be so enormous, organizations devote a significant amount of energy and effort to tightly controlling and managing this marketing-led relationship.

Product brands can be sampled and quality controlled—the characteristics of each bottle of Coke, packet of Persil, or tube of Colgate should be exactly as designed. A product can be picked off the production line and tested. If it isn't as it should be, production can be halted until it is.

Service brands

A service brand is a brand where the customer benefit is essentially inseparable from the service associated with the brand. While product brands are tangible, visible things, service brands are intangible and invisible. Nonetheless, they very much exist.

People *like* brands. Product brands may be likeable for all sorts of reasons. Service brands are also likeable, sometimes for more profound or more emotional reasons.

One reason why we like service brands is that just as with product brands, they are likely to give us a sense of familiarity, of belonging, a sense of community in a world that can feel like a lonely place to be.

Try this experiment: the next time you are in the center of the town you live in, visit a branch of a bank that is not your own bank branch and spend a few minutes there. Your "mental map" of your town center will change slightly, or even significantly; even the aspect of the High Street from inside the unfamiliar branch will look different. You will feel different. You are no longer quite on home territory.

Service brands, in contrast to product brands, cannot be sampled and quality controlled in the same way because they are intangible. Their characteristics cannot be encapsulated simply by product specification, price, place, and promotion because there is an experiential element to service brands. Product specifications in service businesses, such as the components of insurance policies or savings accounts can be copied overnight; prices can be matched; and distribution and promotions of service features are, at best, short-lived differentiators.

Nor can service brands be promoted independently of the organization supplying them. Customers simply cannot separate what they feel about the organization from what they feel about its (intangible) products. Indeed, customers would not relate to terms such as the "long-haul product" or the "fixed-term product," to use the kind of phrases employed within the marketing departments of an airline or a bank, respectively. Customers understand the experience of flying or of banking with a particular organization—and, form a view of the organization based on their current and past experience of the company and its competitors, on word of mouth, as well as on the promise as promoted through the organization's marketing.

The challenge of differentiating service brands is far more complex than differentiating product brands as is illustrated by Figure 2.

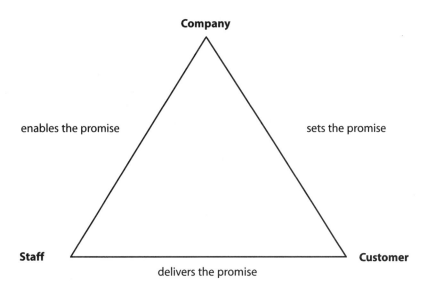

Figure 2 The service triangle

While a (service) company still sets a promise to its customers through its marketing proposition—the four Ps—down the right-hand side of the triangle, the delivery of that promise happens when the customer interacts with customer-facing staff (the base of the triangle). Indeed, customers don't know what they are going to get until they themselves are involved—the customer is using the service as it is being produced. When a customer approaches a cashier in a bank the nature of the service delivered (the delivery of the promise) depends totally on the skills, attitude, and behavior of the employee, plus the systems and processes that support them. Further, the customer him or herself shapes the experience—he or she is part of the final production process.

In service businesses, what dominates customers' views of the company are the interactions they have with front-line staff. Indeed, our research over the last ten years has shown that between 70 percent or 80 percent of their view is conditioned by these interactions—the attitude of the contact center agent; the helpfulness of the cashier or booking clerk. The remaining 20 percent to 30 percent is related to the traditional 4Ps of marketing. Yet, what percentage of most board-room debates and budgetary considerations go to products and marketing issues as opposed to ensuring the ability of front-line staff in delivering impressive customer experiences?

The dilemma for management in service organizations is that their brand is dynamic—it is delivered at the customer interface, and even if they do realize the value of their customer-facing staff, as many today do, they cannot control the perceived value that their customers have of their brand. It's the way we feel about our experience rather than any objective measure that makes the difference.

The service brand is in the hands of often hundreds or thousands of staff who are delivering perhaps tens of thousands of relatively small interactions. And it is at each and every one of these interactions that customers are, often subconsciously, deciding what they feel about the company and its brand. Of course, the price and cover of a travel insurance policy play a part—but to the customer, travel insurance is widely available and "all the same"—so the experience delivered by the insurance company's agent will be the deciding factor.

Let's look at an example of a company competing in the emerging market of fitness and well-being, Holmes Place. Holmes Place is an award winner for customer service in a crowded and competitive marketplace. Over the last 15 years there has been a social trend prompting an increasing desire for customers to improve their fitness, figures, and physiques as well as use an increasing range of beauty treatments—for both men and women. The market to meet customers' needs is—some would say—saturated.

But customer intentions are not always in line with their commitment, and customer churn in this market is significant—two-thirds of customers who join a gym don't last the course. The challenge for companies like Holmes Place is to retain their customers and increase the range of value-added services the customers can consume. Holmes Place has found that the best way to make this happen is to ensure the gym feels like a club. Lesley Cotton, the Human Resources director of Holmes Place, explains:

> *Customers do feel virtuous after visiting the gym and it's the job of all our staff to make sure customers feel really good about themselves. Our people can set us apart. The way we achieve this is by focusing on service as a key differentiator of the experiences that customers have at Holmes Place. The initial part is to make sure our members feel really comfortable—and our people have a key role in establishing the friendliness, the clubbable element. From our front desk receptionists (we call them service consultants) to instructors to cleaners, everyone has a role in this. Plus increasing*

98

the feeling of being part of a club is something our people recognize as incredibly important to success. It's achieved by ensuring we make our service experience visible to customers. Obviously we have to start with our basic operational standards and checks but we also concentrate on the service experience through our GUEST programme which focuses on how greetings and body language can make customers feel connected to the club.

Sometimes the points at which a service brand is consumed, however, will be such that no particular human interaction is taking place at all. For example, a customer in a queue at a retail bank who spots a leaflet advertising the retail bank's new family travel insurance policy and reads the leaflet while in the queue, is in a very real sense interacting with this particular service brand. Of course, when the customer gets home and makes a telephone enquiry about the family travel insurance policy, a very different kind of interaction will take place, but both types of interaction are, in their own way, significant.

In fact research at the direct bank First Direct—the UK's most recommended bank—showed that customers can be impressed with a service brand where personal service does not necessarily imply access to service providers. Customers can "self serve" (see Chapter 9) most successfully and as a preference, but still feel loyal to the service brand. Matthew Higgins, the head of brand planning and communications, describes it this way:

Our research shows that personal doesn't necessarily mean you always have to talk to a person. In fact our e-banking customers are more satisfied even though they have less personal contact. But they know with First Direct that they can get through to a person if they need to. Ultimately they trust us not to leave them in the lurch.

For many companies, of course, the importance of their customer-facing staff in the customer interaction is paramount and they invest in their training and ongoing development. But what is so rarely fully appreciated are the vitally important factors that enable—or not—staff to deliver the promise, as represented by the left-hand side of the service triangle (Figure 2). These factors that enable staff to deliver the quality and value of the brand are:

- The climate of the organization—does it support and encourage staff to deliver high quality experiences to customers?

- The morale and motivation of staff.
- How people are managed—are they encouraged and developed to believe that giving an impressive customer experience is vital to their own and to the company's success?
- Business measures—as always, what gets measured gets done. If the customer experience is to be seen as truly important then it must be a Key Performance Indicator for staff, for business units, and for the organization as a whole, alongside other measures.

What this means, and is indicated by the Service Triangle, is that the brand experience in service organizations must be seen as a company-wide issue. In Heskett, Sasser, and Schlesinger's 1997 bestseller *The Service Profit Chain*, they make the point that although it is entirely appropriate that organizations place a great deal of emphasis on the challenge of producing successful service encounters, this could prove an expensive distraction. Too much research, they argue, has focused on the front line when it is the broader strategic decisions of which the service experience is to some extent an outcome. It overlooks the fact that effectiveness of front-line service must be the responsibility of top management.

Hence the design and delivery of the brand cannot be the responsibility of one or two parts of the organization—they must be looked at holistically. This, again, adds a complexity that does not exist in product-based organizations where marketing, sales, human resources (HR), finance, and operations can all operate neatly in departmental silos, each typically reporting to a senior executive. This "traditional" organizational structure works fine when the focus of the business is about delivering its products profitably to customers because the business tasks can be subdivided into these functions and each can succeed, more or less, independently of the others. One silo is responsible for selling; another for manufacturing; a third for distribution, and so on. And staff issues, as covered by HR, are purely internal in a product-based business—they do not impact on the customer because the staff do not, in the main, impact on the customer.

When translated to a service business, the traditional approach to structuring the organization causes difficulties because the focus of the business is about delivering intangible experiences—not tangible products—profitably to customers, which requires many more departments or functions to work seamlessly together. However, we still see service businesses where sales and after-sales (often, ironically, called "customer service") are managed separately, with different objectives and reporting to different senior executives. This can lead to practices where sales staff—driven by sales targets—rush customers off the phone with little care for anything other than getting the deal.

Little surprise that when the after-sales staff pick up the contact, the customer feels little allegiance to the company (and the brand) and is disinclined to buy more or stay with the company, let alone say that the experience would lead him or her to talk favorably about the company. Similarly, most organizations with both a branch network and contact centers manage the two functions separately. What typically happens is that the branch network is managed for maximizing sales, with staff encouraged to give customers time and to build relationships; and the contact center is managed to minimize costs, with staff discouraged from giving customers time! Thus the organizational silos leads directly to the customer getting an inconsistent brand experience.

As can be seen in the service triangle, the factors depicted by the left-hand side of the triangle cut across many silos—not just these customer-facing departments, as illustrated above. The HR policies that determine staff performance, management, and reward systems; the management information reported to the executive by the finance department; these are, in effect, enablers of the successful delivery of the brand. Everyone has a role, and if each person does not recognize this and minimize the pitfalls of silos as created by a traditional organizational structure, the experience for customers will be sub-optimal.

In summary, all customer-facing functions, such as sales and after-sales, need to be managed in a way that creates the desired experience consistently for the desired customer types—irrespective of the point of contact. In addition, many other departments that would not have seen their role as having an external, customer impact—such as HR, training, even finance—need to recognize the enabling effect their department has on the customer-facing functions and align their own functions accordingly. This need for greater synergy across departments is leading to the introduction, often at a quite senior level, of appointments in many major service businesses of "customer experience" executives who have the role of breaking down the silos and endeavoring to get different departments to work together to enable customer-facing staff to deliver the organization's desired customer promise.

The pressing need for clarity

If, as we argue, it is each and every interaction with each and every customer that conveys the quality and value of the service brand, it follows that customer-facing staff must be given total clarity about how the organization wants the customer to feel and their role in delivering this. Again, let's refer to the experience of First Direct:

> *The essence of our brand is Expect Respect—to and from customers. We encourage our people to try to recognize the customer's mood; while staying professional. We don't use the customer's first name but we do expect our people to be able to adjust their responses to vary speed, empathy and pick up on a customer's concerns. Our style is not as "quirky" as some of the new players—there is still a professional distance. We don't use service scripts and never have done—we want our people to have conversations with customers. It's an adult-to-adult relationship though, not a parent to child.*

Furthermore, First Direct has defined which types of customers value their proposition, so that the right experience is delivered to the right people. The purpose is, after all, about delivering a service to customers—profitably.

But of course not all consumers are the same and—depending upon a range of factors such as how knowledgeable they believe themselves to be about the service; how experienced they are at buying this type of service, and so on—they require a different mindset from the member of staff with whom they are dealing.

For customer-facing staff this is, to a point, common sense and something they naturally adapt to—but only to a point. They can tell if the customer wants to chat or simply get things done and move on; whether the customer wants a lot of detailed information or not. However, the temptation of marketing departments is to do market research and produce a sophisticated segmentation analysis defining many complex buying behaviors of their customers and hope that customer-facing departments can adopt these definitions and improve their performance.

One organization has developed 125 customer segments which may help with their direct marketing activity but, not surprisingly, such a sophisticated analysis cannot be used by those dealing directly with customers because it cannot be "operationalized," however accurate it may be.

At the point of delivery, staff can recognize and adopt different behavioral techniques with perhaps up to six different customer types; no more. To get staff to embrace this concept, target customers should be easy to identify, and not shrouded in tricky names. They should be simple enough for everyone in the organization to understand and relate to. Targets might be "teenagers" or "first-time buyers" for example, where everyone can picture a teenager, or identify a first-time buyer with one simple question. The more recognizable the target market segments, the more likely the organization can understand the vision and effectively deliver the right experience to the right customers.

There is, after all, little commercial sense in selling to customers who could have been predicted to be "butterflies." A bland vision statement is not enough, staff need:

- an inspiring rallying call that tells them just how important their interactions with customers are to the business
- to know which customers the company is aiming to win and keep
- to understand what an excellent experience would feel like for the customer
- the skills and behaviors to deliver this experience, each and every time they interact with the customer
- to be managed and motivated in a way that reinforces the importance of delivering this experience, each and every day.

As we have described, customers of service organizations may interact with many individuals within a company across their "lifetime" of being a customer, and at each interaction they are making a judgment about the quality and value of the company and its brand. Whilst these interactions may be infrequent, they may well be happening over some considerable time and potentially across a number of different channels—in branches, over the telephone, by mail, or the Internet.

The concept of "moments of truth" introduced by Jan Carlson of the airline SAS over 20 years ago is still relevant today. Customers do not logically evaluate the experience at these touchpoints against some mental checklist, it is all about how they feel. Companies need to understand where it matters to the customer, where the key touchpoints are, and design the experience—irrespective of the channel—to convey the quality and value of the brand.

When a customer deals initially with a branch of, say, a mortgage provider, the detailed discussion he or she has with the advisor should—if handled well—leave the customer feeling impressed with the experience and hence with the organization itself. If, as so often happens, the customer subsequently has cause to phone the organization, his or her expectations of the person they are going to deal with are high. The opportunity to, in some way, let the customer down is far greater than if there had been no other point of contact. As customers we see the organization as one entity and expect a seamless experience—the complexities of different channels, under different management structures, are not our concern.

By ensuring staff understand what an excellent experience would feel like for the customer and that they can articulate their own role in delivering it gives them clarity of their role and sets boundaries. Many organizations talk of the need to empower staff—indeed, an excellent experience cannot be delivered without empowering and encouraging staff to take personal responsibility. But staff will not change their behavior simply because they are told "Customer satisfaction is our number one priority," or, worse still, "The customer is king." They need to know what they can do for the customer and what they cannot do. They need clarity, guidance boundaries.

If a customer calls a contact center about a non-standard insurance risk; or to ask for a charge on his or her bank account to be reversed, or to change the payments on his or her mortgage, does the agent have the authority to handle it? Or does he or she have to elevate the customer to a more senior person? Either can be effective for the customer—as long as the agent has clarity and knows the boundaries. What all too often happens is the agent believes he or she cannot answer the point, cannot find someone who can, and makes an insincere promise that something will happen or someone will call the customer back.

If a customer calls First Direct to say that he or she has been charged for going overdrawn and that it is the first time it has happened, the agent has information to be able to see if it really is the first time; has authority to reverse the charge if so, or knows to tell the customer that it has happened before, so the charge stands. The agent has clarity and understands the boundaries.

Service brands and customer loyalty

The customer loyalty issue facing organizations supplying service brands is so complex that it deserves to have a book written about it. In fact, there have been several books written on this subject, and of course you are reading one of them.

The basic reason why the customer loyalty issue relating to service brands is so complex is that—almost by definition—service brands are not one-off experiences, as product brands tend to be. Instead, service brands will be judged on an essentially ongoing basis at the many points of interaction between the service brand and the customer. And there's the rub.

Service brands are especially challenging to management because service experiences are continually evaluated. Human experiences cannot be evaluated objectively in absolute terms as "good or bad." Instead we judge them against other factors.

As customers, when we consider whether we like a meal, a holiday, a haircut, the quality of advice we're given, inevitably we are making a comparison. Social scientist Alex Michalos in his discussion of the perceived quality of experience argues that people establish standards based on the assessment of three gaps:

- the gap between what one has and what one wants
- the gap between what one has and things others like oneself has, and
- the gap between what one has and the best one has had in the past.

The third gap—that between what one has and the best one has had in the past—creates a particular challenge for service businesses; and is especially important because the comparisons influence our decisions about what we'll do in the future.

It is the result of a key characteristic of human nature—our capacity to adapt and to adapt quickly. Simply put, we get used to things and then we start to take them for granted. To psychologists it's known as "hedonic adaptation." ("Hedonic" is a term used in psychology to convey the idea of pertaining to pleasure.)

An interesting example of hedonic adaptation was a survey in which respondents were asked to rate their happiness on a five-point scale. Some of the respondents had won between $50 000 and $1 million on lotteries. Other respondents had become paraplegic or quadriplegic as

105

a result of accidents. Not surprisingly, lottery winners were happier than those who had been paralyzed. What was surprising though was that lottery winners were no happier than people in general, and accident victims, while somewhat less happy than people in general, still judged themselves to be happy.

What happens in hedonic adaptation is explained by two reasons. First, people just get used to things. Second, new experiences (good or bad) set new standards against which experiences are judged.

There is good and bad news in this for service business problems caused by our human ability to adapt. The bad news is that because of adaptation, what we used to think of as impressive—access to 24-hour banking for example—becomes a new norm. An organization can only hope to sustain the brand if it can consistently meet exacting standards. This means working very hard and having to operate all the time at the very wavefront of superb service.

The good news is that when your customers have adapted to your organization's high standards of service, and if you can succeed in truly impressing them, they will be less tempted to risk a potential disappointment by switching to an organization whose standard of standard is unfamiliar to them.

In other words, get the service proposition associated with your service brands right, and there is every reason why you might keep your customer indefinitely.

6   The one question that really matters

Roberto—the customer loyalty guru

Every year a friend of ours travels with her family to a small Italian sea-side resort on the Adriatic coast. They always go in the same week for a short May holiday which they like to regard as marking the end of the winter and the start of the summer.

As is usually the case in that part of Italy, access to the stunning sea is divided into a great many private beach clubs. These all provide rented sunshades, sunbeds, food, drink, and children's play facilities to anyone wishing to spend the day at the beach. Every beach club is a separate business, usually operated by a family concern. Every club is about the same size, accommodating around 300–400 sun seekers at any one time. Ostensibly the only visible differentiator between the clubs (apart from their names) is the color of the umbrellas or perhaps the lunchtime special advertised on the blackboard in the café.

The year when our friend and her family began visiting the resort, they chanced upon a beach club known as Bagno Sorriso, one of 20 or so beach clubs all within an easy walk of their hotel. They were greeted by the owner of the club, Roberto, who through the language barrier enquired where they would like to sit. Roberto, noticing the younger members of the family, asked our friend whether the family preferred to be nearer to the sea or to the play facilities and café. My friend explained where the family most liked to sit and Roberto paid careful attention. Throughout all the holiday Roberto was attentive in this way, and did not press for daily payments. Indeed, money was scarcely discussed at all; he did not ask for this and was happy to leave things until the end of the week. After a wonderful holiday—and a daily friendly wave from Roberto, always busy among his many cus-tomers—my friend settled the perfectly reasonable bill and left Bagno Sorriso to go home, full of happy memories of the break.

Over the following few years, my friend and her family continued to choose Bagno Sorriso, always receiving the same warm and friendly reception from Roberto and his colleagues. Each day the family spent money in the café; drinks, breakfast, occasionally lunch. Some years they brought other friends and relatives along to holiday with them at the resort who did the same.

Then one year something extraordinary happened. Rather than travel in their usual week at the end of May, our friend and her family traveled one week later, in June. Arriving at the Bagno Sorriso there was the customary warm welcome, then Roberto—in his halting English—remarked, "What happened? We were expecting you last week."

Roberto was making a joke but you can imagine the effect his remark had. Among hundreds of customers in the course of a week, among thousands of customers in the course of a season, Roberto had noticed that a "regular customer" had not turned up when expected.

Roberto is a clever man, and a great winner of customer loyalty. He builds relationships with individuals, with families, with their friends, and friends of friends. His business depends upon it, since his product is virtually indistinguishable from literally hundreds of similar beach clubs that run the length of the coastline. For our friend, the family's conversations with Roberto are an integral part of their holiday. Roberto has secured their loyalty—forever.

It is on the face of it entirely obvious that the only way to grow a company is to win more customers, to keep them coming back, and to bring more business through recommendations and referrals. What is a matter of intense debate, however, is exactly *how* customer loyalty will be won. Addressing this question involves formulating answers to some fundamental questions about human nature. One of the most important ones is this: do people prefer familiarity and stability or novelty and change?

Twenty or thirty years ago, changing one's supplier used to be the ultimate indication that a customer was dissatisfied. Changing the supplier could be a momentous matter; many customers of retail banks, for example, would never change their bank at all; or perhaps just once in a lifetime. Customers' habits of being supplied by a particular organization died hard; and quite apart from anything else customers' access to information about what else was available in the marketplace was pretty much limited to what different organizations said about themselves. At a purely practical level, to step into the unknown and find a new insurance broker, bank, or even retailer involved the customer in some considerable effort. Even if there were other players on the other side of the High Street, the process of changing over to them was long and complicated, and for a bank would involve an interview with a bank manager in which the customer was as likely to be "auditioning" as the bank itself was.

Nowadays, thanks to sources of information such as consumer "best buy" magazines, "league tables" comparing performance between different players, and of course the Internet, comparing suppliers' products and services features is simplicity itself. Indeed, most organizations even promote their services to customers by offering to take on the process of switching themselves—credit cards, mortgages, utilities to name a few. Interestingly, companies also often advertise that they'll help customers "come back"—implying, in a way, that customers must have been stupid to leave them.

But despite all the incentives today that tempt customers to be disloyal, there is every reason to believe that, in fact, the crucial point we made at the very beginning of this book still most definitely applies. Yes, customers *want* to remain loyal. Certainly they need to feel themselves overwhelmed with reasons why they *should* remain loyal, but the fact they *want* to find those reasons appears incontestable, even today.

Well, perhaps we can understand it. After all, customers are dealing with a commercial environment where continually comparing rates, suppliers, and remaining constantly vigilant to the risk of being "ripped off" all represent a great deal of extra effort in already busy lives. Plus, there's no easy way to anticipate and predict what treatment the customer will receive in the hands of a new supplier.

In our experience, the customers we have met don't want to spend their spare time working as hard as this. Most normal human beings attempt to avoid anxiety and uncertainty if they can; this avoidance is part of human nature. This explains why loyalty to a trusted organization is something people are willing to give—provided they are willing to trust the supplier they choose to take great care of them. This leads on to the reason why organizations must strive to deliver an experience which convinces customers that they couldn't do any better and that is worth the price. Our research has confirmed time and time again that many customers want to stay put in the "loyalty situation" which they are already occupying. When they are impressed with their supplier, they have no reason to leave, just as people have no reason to leave a marriage or serious relationship just as long as they are in love with their spouse or partner and are happy.

Despite these commonsense observations about customer loyalty, a great many writers on customer loyalty today argue that customers *don't* want to be loyal. They present evidence of sectors' churn rates (30 to 60 percent in many sectors), and claim this alone proves that customers are intrinsically fickle and happy to shop around. We believe this is wrong. We also believe very firmly that just because *some* customers clearly are very interested in shopping around, this does not mean that *most* customers are. Too many writers on customer loyalty fail to make basic observations about human nature. And it is human nature, we would argue, essentially to want to be loyal.

Our belief is that customers want to be loyal to organizations which win their trust and confidence. If relationships with customers make customers feel this way, then being loyal to that organization makes their lives easier. It's an antidote to the stresses caused by some of the trends described in Chapter 3 of this book, which impact the way we live and the choices we make.

The emotional links between customer loyalty and friendship

There appears to be considerable similarity, at an emotional level, between the loyalty we feel to organizations we like (that is, that have impressed us) and the loyalty we feel to friends.

In his thought-provoking book *The Paradox of Choice* (2004), Barry Schwartz observes:

> *We are drawn to people who meet our standards for intelligence, kindness, character, loyalty, wit and then we stick with them. We don't make a choice every day about whether to maintain the friendship, we just do.*

What is true of the choices we make when we choose our friends is also true of the choices we make when we choose organizations to which we want to be loyal. We *want* to stick with organizations we like, just as we want to stick with people we like.

Returning to the social trends identified in Chapter 3, let's analyze them in terms of their implications for an organization's ability to impress customers.

Interconnected individualism

In general, when customers have been impressed with a supplier, they feel good about it. Usually this makes them only too happy to pass on their tips and advice to others. The emotional motivation to share such thoughts and experiences is the desire to win the approval or the gratitude of others; it feeds self-esteem. Remember when you last saw a movie you really liked? Didn't you recommend it wholeheartedly to many of your friends, colleagues, and relatives because you wanted the pleasure of them sharing in your own appreciation of it?

The permanent hurry

"At the Bank of Ireland, our customer research in July 2004 found queues in the branches to be a big concern for customers," says Brian Lande, head of customer service at the Bank of Ireland. Has the permanent hurry hit Ireland, a country with a worldwide reputation for a rather more pleasant pace of life? In fact, time spent in queues was the number one issue with customers. Bank of Ireland has responded by doubling the number of its ATMs but also by putting its people back into branches. "If our customers want face-to face service, they should be able to access it," Lande says.

Time is precious and not to be wasted. The idea that a customer really wants to spend any of it switching suppliers is only accurate when a customer feels that something is missing from the relationship with his or her current supplier or that something has gone wrong: Perhaps the customer believes or is persuaded that there is a better financial deal around the corner. Much more commonly in our experience, customers do not believe there is any relationship to speak of in the first place, and believe that to spend time shopping around for a new supplier is "what they're expected to do."

The trust implosion

Traditional advertising and marketing techniques are losing their effectiveness. Not only are many customers increasingly cynical about marketing messages (which is hardly surprising, as marketing messages are so obviously driven by a very obvious commercial self-interest), but also a dispersed and crowded media marketplace means getting customers' attention is doubly hard.

People are more likely to trust people they know and listen to the thoughts and experiences of people they respect. For this reason word of mouth is now recognized as increasingly important. Additionally, the trust implosion causes customers to question whether it is really worth switching suppliers or whether it will prove a pain but no gain.

Ethic-quette

Customers are increasingly likely to be swayed by ethical considerations when deciding to which organizations they offer their loyalty. This growing trend may in fact be linked to the feeling many people have that traditional moral constants are fading in societies that often seem to be a moral free-for-all. Certainly, organizations that do adhere to certain specific ethical considerations and actively promote this adherence often find they win additional levels of customer loyalty as a result. In the United Kingdom, for example, the Co-operative Bank won considerable success when it decided only to invest in organizations that met certain ethical considerations it set down.

The fact that customers do appear to be influenced by ethical issues is not only an important commercial observation; it is surely also encouraging from the point of view of the moral development of society.

Rude rage

This is also directly related to the previous point. Customers' expectations are rising and consumer power has sensitized customers to the way they are treated in many different interactions. There is, perhaps, too much rudeness and gratuitous informality in society today, and organizations that take steps to prevent themselves being infected with this problem are, other things being equal, likely to harvest benefits.

An obvious example is the extensive and even almost automatic use of first names by contact center agents when they talk to customers for the first time. Many customers do not like this, or at the very least prefer to be asked first whether being addressed by their first name is acceptable. It certainly creates a friendlier climate than using, for example, "Mr Smith" each time, but it may be felt to be too informal, especially for customers who are obviously significantly older than the contact center agent.

For interactions outside the English-speaking world, another consideration here is whether the contact center agent feels entitled to use the informal or formal 'you', such as *tu/vous* in French and *du/Sie* in German. Again, tact and consideration are necessary here, and just because it may be easier and quicker for the contact center agent to use the customer's first name and the informal "you" does not necessarily mean that the customer will appreciate it. As with everything in this book, it is the customer's agenda that should be taken as the primary one, not the organization's.

In fact, this subject is another argument that bolsters the advantages of winning loyalty, because when the organization really knows the customer, it will know what the customer's preferences really are as far as formality are concerned. And so from a customer perspective, remaining loyal to an organization that "gets to know its customers" minimizes the need to repeat personal information and preferences, being bombarded with inappropriate cross-sells, or of being treated "rudely."

Stressfulness of choice

The American psychologist Barry Schwartz has published research suggesting that an over-abundance of choice can actually reduce our decision-making capacity and even cause depression.

Certainly, we are all likely to have anecdotal evidence that choice is often hard work. Going clothes and accessory shopping on Saturday may be enjoyable, but it also brings with it certain stresses; not the least of which is wondering whether this or that really suits us; whether we have made the right choice.

Search for authenticity

One of the best examples of companies' lack of understanding of customers' desire for authenticity in relationships concerns research we undertook for one of the UK's biggest retail banks. In focus groups we had asked customers how they would show loyalty to a bank and a great many explained that for them, the most authentic gesture of loyalty they could make was when they took a child into a bank to start a lifetime's consumption of financial services. Almost universally these customers described being dismissed off-handedly with a sheaf of leaflets and forms to complete at home. What was the reason? There were no sales rewards associated with opening a child's account and staff were therefore very unwilling to invest any time in doing so.

To take another example, Laithwaites is the world's largest mail order wine company. In our view, Laithwaites is as authentically passionate about its customers' experience as it is about its wines. In

113

2004 the company began to focus in earnest on retention, and developing a low churn-business model. Although it has grown through a total of 60 partners (such as BA, Halifax and the National Trust) it realized that it ran the risk of switching customers from one partner to other, not growing the business.

The goal was to ensure the customers enjoyed the experience of dealing with Laithwaites so that the experience became more enjoyable than a merely placing an order. It was important to get it across that this was because the company was *not* trying to develop a lowest-cost means of contact—its staff wanted to really talk with its customers. Laithwaites tapped into its staff's motivation and aspirations in building the low turnover model. Victoria Sherston, head of customer operations, explains:

> *We asked staff to say what would this mean. They told us it was all about the appropriateness of the conversation to make the contact experience better. Our people told us, for example, that the information they had to ask customers was inappropriate—so we changed it (in the past we asked things we wanted to know from a marketing prospective—but that's not always good from an experience perspective). Talking about wine isn't easy, and we all agreed we didn't want our people to start talking about our wines in a patronizing or in an insincere—"hint of blackberry" or "on the nose"—sort of way. We knew we must avoid pretentious language but wanted our operators (a.k.a. our contact centre agents) to be real product advocates. Our goal is that our people convey such an enthusiasm for wine that our customers rip open the delivery boxes with excitement. We've found it's anecdotes and stories that create this feeling, not wine talk.*
>
> *Growing the knowledge and enthusiasm of our people is achieved by having our wine buyers, writers and suppliers run "Wine Alive" sessions for our operators, and everyone attends one every month. We train them with authentic anecdotes about specific wines, not to use pretentious wine language our customers would find ridiculous. In particular, all our people are fully trained on knowing about what we call our "20 Hero Wines." These are the wines we are most actively promoting at any time. In practice, our staff are encouraged to talk about our wines in their own words because we want them to use their individual personalities. For example, one of our wines, the XV du President, is grown in an area of southern France. Our people can tell our customers that the rugby team there drink it at half time!*

> *Getting the right feelings across about Laithwaites is tremendously important to us. Many of our customers think we're small—we build on this, but it takes real organization. For example we can do a mailing to 18 500 customers and someone will call us saying, "It's Teresa Smith of Tunbridge Wells—you've really tempted me with that Chablis!" We can't reply by asking the customer, "What's your customer number?" or "What offer number are you referring to?" The customer expects us to know and it's our job to make sure they feel we do.*
>
> *We have definitely found it to be an advantage that we are perceived as a small company. If, for example we failed to answer a customer's call because our centre is busy, we capture numbers and we call that customer back to apologize. We feel we have earned the right to the close relationship we have with our customers.*

Customers—who are human beings after all—want to deal with people and organizations they like and whom they believe like them.

The point is that we all know how complex, chaotic, and ultimately indifferent the world is to us and to our hopes, dreams, and ambitions. Yet despite this we want to belong; we want to feel that the people and organizations to which we give our business actually care about us and our individual needs. When customers get that feeling, they become loyal.

The Loyalty Effect

You have probably already undertaken some good hard thinking about your customers and what you're doing to win the loyalty they're prepared to invest. You're in good company. Since American guru Frederich F. Reichheld published his highly influential and best-selling books, *The Loyalty Effect* (1996) and *Loyalty Rules* (2001), businesses are paying more attention to loyalty generation than they have ever done in the past.

Reichheld's books make an aggressive and powerful case for the principle that winning customer loyalty is far too important to be seen as a mere adjunct to what an organization should be doing. He argues that winning customer loyalty is absolutely the be-all and end-all of why an organization is in business. Because of this, he believes the objective of winning customer loyalty should be built into every part of an organization's operations. Furthermore, Reichheld—using a wide range of case studies—convincingly establishes the link between loyalty and bottom-line profits: a link we ourselves explored in Chapter 4.

The organizations that really want success now and lasting success in the future are taking on board the following crucially important beliefs, and are acting on them with passion, energy, and creativity:

- The drive for customer loyalty is too important to be delegated to a marketing department.
- The responsibility for maximizing the customer loyalty that an organization wins sits fairly and squarely with the chief executive officer (CEO).
- Winning and maintaining customer loyalty deserves the same kind of attention that is lavished on such issues as stock price, cash flow, and regulatory compliance.
- Customer loyalty should have a fundamental dynamic effect on every element of an organization's business operations; it drives business success and therefore CEO careers.
- Consistently high customer retention stemming from winning customer loyalty can create tremendous competitive advantage, boost employee morale, produce fundamental bonuses in productivity and growth, and even reduce the cost of capital.

Conversely, organizations from which customers persistently defect because they are convinced the organization offers inferior value will soon find that these defecting customers outnumber the organization's loyal advocates and may even dominate the collective voice of the marketplace. If this occurs, no amount of advertising, public relations, or clever marketing will be likely to save the organization's reputation.

The US experience is decisively in favor of the principle that organizations that take customer loyalty seriously are much more likely to get taken seriously by existing and potential customers than those that do not. It demonstrates that organizations winning significant levels of loyalty from their customers do not do so by accident or by good fortune but because they set customer loyalty firmly in their sights as something to be achieved and devote themselves to achieving it.

After conducting extensive practical research, Reichheld has concluded that the acid test of whether a customer truly feels loyal to an organization or not is to ask the customer, "Would you recommend this organization to a friend, relative or colleague?" This question has proved itself to be significantly more reliable than any other, more complex, criteria for assessing customer loyalty.

Reichheld assesses customers' willingness to recommend an organization using an ascending scale of 0 to 10. Those customers willing to endorse 9 or 10 on the scale, he regards as "promoters" of the organization. These are customers who are really fired with enthusiasm for the organization and would recommend it spontaneously. Reichheld sees customers who register 7 or 8 as "passive" and those who score 6 or less as "detractors." He uses the three categories to calculate his Net Promoter score, by subtracting the percentage of detractors from that of promoters. The larger the result, the more likely that an organization is growing profitably—since the number of customers actively recommending the business to others exceeds those that feel less enthusiastic.

Reichheld's research does seem to bear out what observation of the real business—and indeed sheer common sense—suggests: that truly loyal customers, by recommending a particular organization, product, or service by word of mouth, can in effect amount to an unpaid sales force for that organization.

The US experience also clearly indicates that there is an intimate, even symbiotic, relationship between customer loyalty and employee loyalty: that it is likely to be impossible to maintain a loyal customer base without a base of loyal employees. Furthermore, the symbiosis between customer loyalty and employee loyalty also includes investor loyalty, because winning employee loyalty is in practice difficult if the owners of the business are indifferent to employee needs.

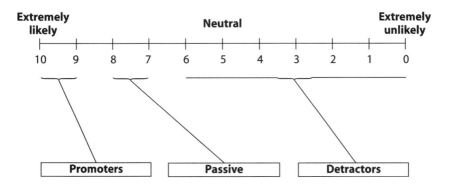

Figure 3a Distribution over the 0 to 10 scores of the Reichheld analysis
Source: Reichheld (2003)

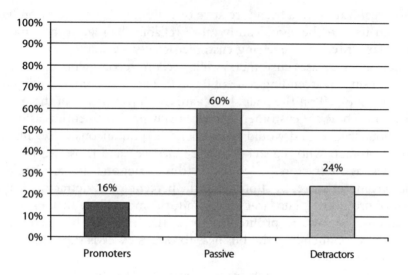

Figure 3b Typical performance in financial services

As Reichheld himself comments:

> *Customer retention is a subject that cannot simply be confined within narrow limits.... Business loyalty has three dimensions—customer loyalty, employee loyalty and investor loyalty. They are powerful, far-reaching and interdependent. Loyalty has implications that extend into every corner of every business system that seeks the benefit of steady customers. Tempting as it may be to delegate customer retention to the marketing department, what can marketing do to stem the outflow of employees and investors?*

And Reichheld adds:

> *Stemming the customer exodus is not simply a matter of marketing: it demands a reconsideration of core strategy and operating principles. Loyalty provides the unifying framework that enables an executive team to modify and integrate corporate strategy and operating practices in ways that will better serve the long-term interests of customers, employees and investors. Even more importantly, the loyalty framework permits a set of practical measures that executives can use to manage the company's value creation process, the upstream source of all profits and growth.*

Winning recommendations through loyalty-building experiences (LBEs)

"The Bank of Ireland has grown the last 14 years in a row. Yet customers seem to see a fundamental conflict in bottom-line performance versus investment in them as customers," says the Bank of Ireland's Brian Lande. "I think our 2004 research revealed the root of this feeling—a big concern for customers is a perceived lack of recognition for their loyalty." He continues, "At the Bank of Ireland, we feel we've done the cost-cutting and the sales improvements part and yes, customer service has improved. But there's more to do in making sure everything is designed to work together for the real benefit of the customer."

The Bank of Ireland's strategy for keeping its customers loyal combines continual process improvements with a thorough and specific customer service programme detailing how each service interaction should *feel*. And it's far-reaching, covering every touchpoint in the customers' experience.

So what practical steps can an organization take to stem the customer exodus? At Cape Consulting, we base our practical interventions on the belief—borne out again and again by experience—that, other things being equal, customer loyalty derives straightforwardly and entirely from the customer service experience customers enjoy.

Ultimately, there is a simple but momentous logical sequence that links quality of customer service with generation of customer loyalty and profitability. This logical sequence is: customers who are impressed with the service they experience from an organization are likely to:

- buy more of the same—indefinitely
- buy other things—indefinitely
- enthusiastically recommend it to their relatives, friends, business contacts, and anyone else who matters in their lives.

This fundamental point connects the quality of customer service experiences with commercial performance. When customers remain loyal, costs go down and profits go up. To measure loyalty, successful companies pay close attention to the Net Promoter score. Measuring customer loyalty is important because loyalty is the key to predictable profits. If you don't understand and can't measure the things that

119

inspire customer loyalty, you won't be able to adjust your services to turn your passive customers into promoters.

What practical assistance can be given to organizations that want to transform the level of customer service they offer to customers? At Cape Consulting, our work over the past ten years has identified a range of crucially important experiences which when delivered to a consistently high standard, have an enormously beneficial impact on customers' overall impressions and consequently on the loyalty they extend to the organization.

Cape Consulting's research has identified a total of eight core customer service experiences we call "loyalty-building experiences" (LBEs). Absolutely fundamental to our work here is the assumption that when customers sense a LBE they are significantly more likely to be impressed with the service they are receiving and will, in effect, increase their "likelihood to recommend" by one increment every time they sense that the LBE is present.

When we initially conceived the idea of focusing on these kinds of experience, we were tempted to call them "loyalty-*winning* experiences." But after further careful thought we decided this would wrongly imply each experience alone was sufficient to win a recommendation. The process is more complex than that. To really impress a customer, every LBE must be in evidence; in fact they are co-dependent since impressing a customer sufficiently to turn him or her into a promoter requires holistic effort.

The incidence and effectiveness of LBEs for customers is dependent on the skills, attitudes, and behaviors of a front-line service provider. When your people are talking to customers, it's up to your people to create moments that really impress them. Our research suggests that the best service providers display distinctive characteristics that differentiate them from "the rest" and enable them to routinely deliver such customer experiences—creating promoters.

Interestingly though, these individuals are not necessarily aware of the skills and strategies they use. Sometimes their managers, too, find it difficult to put into words what makes their top performers so effective. We have met many managers who wish they had "more like Jenny or Johnny," implying that the managers sense the special LBE capability of a particular member of staff, but can't articulate it. We hope the LBE tool will, in fact, let them do this.

What makes the interaction governed by LBEs different for customers from those that are not? In general many service experiences are little more than relatively efficient information exchanges and possibly "order taking," rather than being characterized by the factors likely to impress customers and build loyalty. Conversations are constrained by what we've identified as "inhibitors," that is, behaviors on the part of a service provider that actually stop customers feeling impressed. Customers who experience inhibitors when they deal with service providers become at the very best passive customers, in Reichheld's terms. It is however, much more likely that it will be worse than that and they'll become "detractors."

By contrast, we identified that the very best service providers use "accelerators" when they're talking to customers. Our research has shown that some of these behaviors have a strong impact in securing positive customer response and reaction; for example, quickly identifying how willing a customer is to invest time in a conversation. Skilled service providers encourage customers to feel good about their decisions and are comfortable giving—but also receiving—compliments in the course of conversation. Similarly, sharing humor occurs much more frequently in higher caliber service providers and has a positive impact on rapport building with customers. These accelerators actively boost the degree to which customers enjoy the service experience and have a positive impact on likely recommendations and sales.

In practical terms, many organizations find it almost as useful to understand what *not to do* as well as perhaps the skills of high service delivery. This is particularly true for contact centers where typically high turnover rates among staff mean there is almost always a larger percentage of "rookies" than the skilled and experienced. Inhibitors have a particularly damaging effect on a customer's evaluation of a service experience. Examples are not listening to a customer's specific issue, failing to respond to customer emotion, and patronizing or talking down to the customer. Importantly, when inhibitors are present in service interactions, they destroy opportunities for relationship building (value building) even when it has been initiated by the customer. No wonder many customers are inherently disappointed with their customer service experiences.

We believe that the way for organizations to win the customer loyalty war is to focus on ensuring their staff understand and can deliver LBEs. A conversation or encounter peppered with accelerators should be the goal for every service provider every time. Our firm belief is that this is an attainable goal, and that it can cause revolutionary improvements in the quality of an organization's customer service. Even better, these improvements can in the vast majority of cases be achieved without a single penny needing to be spent on capital investment.

The origin of LBEs

Most contacts with an organization are at best efficient but rarely impressive enough to create advocacy or recommendation. Cape Consulting recognized the need to help our clients identify where the opportunities lay to "raise their game," to really impress customers each and every time they made contact. Fundamental to this is a clear definition of what a great customer experience looks like in the mind of the customer—the LBEs.

Over a ten-year period Cape Consulting identified and talked with customers of both UK and international businesses to establish the most common characteristics of an ideal service experience in the eyes of the customer. Based on the findings of both qualitative and quantitative research from more than 40 UK and multinational organizations, the initial list of ideals was extensive, some 50+ factors that customers had identified as important. Many of these were "hygiene" factors that every organization must get right; for example to be "efficient" and "knowledgeable." Through content analysis this list was reduced to a shorter list of 14 discrete elements that if delivered at the highest level would actually impress.

Subsequently extensive quantitative research was conducted with customers based on their experience and evaluation of the 14 elements, to identify which factors most closely correlated to the propensity to recommend the organization; using the Reichheld question:

On a scale of 0–10 where 0 = Extremely unlikely and 10 = Extremely likely: How likely are you to recommend [the organization] to others?

A final list of eight LBEs was devised that can be cross-referenced to Parasuraman's RATER model. Cape Consulting regularly confirms that the eight LBEs remain the most important factors.

The LBEs are more than just a set of words, though! Cape Consulting's research in contact centers has found that customers are more likely to promote products and services if agents deliver high levels of performance in the LBEs. Mediocre performance is insufficient to impress or create perception of a relationship. Further quantitative analysis showed customers must be impressed by service providers for the LBEs to generate a recommendation—in fact only when customers rate LBEs at the maximum 10/10.

The set of eight LBEs are listed below. We use them to gather quantitative research from customers and to assess customer interactions in face-to-face interactions and in contact centers:

LBE 1: "It's easy to access someone who can help."
* Customers want access promptly—either by telephone or face to face.
* Customers always say they should be able to speak with a human being if they wish.

LBE 2: "I spoke to a person who appeared/sounded positive and eager to help."
* Body language and voice should set the tone for the whole interaction by starting well.

LBE 3: "The person I spoke to listened well to what I had to say."
* Customers should be confident that the service provider has paid attention, listened and fully understood.

LBE 4: "I felt I had enough time and did not feel rushed."
* Customers should feel that a conversation is being held at their desired pace and not that of the service provider/agent.

LBE 5: "I got a chance to ask any questions I had."
* Customers have been given the sense that they have time to think, that the duration of an interaction is being run on their terms.

LBE 6: "The person I spoke to seemed to have a good knowledge of what he/she was talking about."
* Customers will reflect their perception of a service provider's knowledge, of both products and systems.

LBE 7: "The person I spoke to at the organization really gave me the impression that he/she enjoyed speaking to me."
* Getting to know the customers is a key factor in conveying the sense that they are valued and appreciated.

LBE 8: "The interaction was concluded to my complete satisfaction."
- Service providers should aim to give customers the impression that it only takes one conversation to resolve the matter and any uncertainty about next steps is eradicated.

Above all, organizations need to remember this: they win customers with the quality of their offerings and their keen pricing, they keep customers by offering them great service. They build major success for the future by sincerely delivering to customers a quality of service that is of such a high standard that customers not only want to recommend the organization, but will positively *insist* on doing so.

We believe the LBEs we have outlined in this chapter, viewed in conjunction with the one question that really matters—whether the customer would recommend the organization to a friend, relative, or colleague—are the real key to winning customer loyalty in today's markets where service brands have risen to prominence. Let's now look at the LBEs in more detail.

7 The loyalty-building experiences take center stage

Customers want to be loyal to organizations that they consider to deserve their loyalty. Why? Because giving such loyalty makes life *easier*—customers don't need to worry about what organization to choose to meet a certain set of needs, and *better*—because they feel they have, as the Carole King song puts it, "got a friend" in their relationship with the organization.

Ideally, a customer wants to be able to feel that the organization is, in an emotional sense, part of the customer's own community of friends. When this happens, the customer's loyalty to the organization can be as strong as his or her loyalty to a close friend.

The crucial importance of loyalty-building experiences (LBEs)

We have argued that our conception of the loyalty-building experience (LBE) is the key to understanding the dynamics of winning customer loyalty in the time-period that really matters to organizations right now: today. This chapter now goes into more detail about the LBEs: those precious techniques for building valued and valuable relationships with customers. There is enormous practical potential for organizations to exploit LBEs to deliver service experiences that impress customers and turn them into promoters.

In essence, LBEs focus on the feelings that an organization wishes to create in customers in order to impress them. It follows from this that the tools service providers can use to create these feelings are all about eliciting an emotional response. What we've learned in deriving our LBEs is incredibly powerful in business and in life.

Furthermore, the use of certain techniques can *accelerate* the degree to which the customer perceives a LBE. In addition, certain behaviors on the part of a service provider will actively inhibit—even stop—customers' positive perceptions and responses from developing. Under those circumstances, there is no way that customers feel impressed enough to become loyal, and so behaviors that accelerate

125

the LBEs are vitally important for service providers to understand and deliver.

The Bank of Ireland's chief executive, Brian Goggin, is creating a bank where customers can "feel the difference." This objective speaks directly to the need to win customers' emotional commitment. As the Bank's Brian Lande points out, "reducing the variability in the performance of our people is the challenge. We need to continually re-energize them. The challenge is to continually motivate the top performers and bring the less skilled ones up. Everyone needs to understand that every time we touch our customers, we are adding or taking away from their experience."

The skills and techniques that deliver the LBEs are tools that our research has shown significantly increase the effectiveness of those who work directly with customers, in either face-to-face or telephone environments. *Many of the techniques we're going to describe are deployed as a matter of course by people we intuitively recognize as warm, likeable, and communicative.*

When it comes to relationship building, most of us have made a few embarrassing mistakes. But just as some of us are better flirts than others, so too are some individuals better at impressing customers. Leaving the relationships that impress and lead to loyalty to service providers' best instincts, however, is obviously not the most effective strategy for organizations. By making the LBEs explicit, observable, and measurable, we have made it possible for the techniques that create them to become teachable. For organizations, it creates the opportunity for service providers to impress more customers, more consistently—a fundamental factor in creating loyalty. Organizations whose customer service staff learn about the LBEs will find themselves at a significant advantage over their rivals in winning customer loyalty.

Loyalty-building experience 1: "It's easy to access someone who can help."

This first loyalty-building feeling will only apply if customers really do feel that the customer service staff member with whom they are interacting really is going to help them. How does a customer know whether this will be so? There is research available suggesting that people's first impressions are based 55 percent on appearance and body language, 38 percent on style of speaking, and only 7 percent on what is actually said. In other words, body language may be the most important "relationship building tool," but vocal signals come a very close second.

The more you think about that 38 percent, the more concerned you should be to ensure that vocal signals—whether face-to-face or when working over the phone—make the best possible impression. Similarly, an ability to "read" the vocal signals of other people helps service providers find out how customers are feeling, how much time they are prepared to invest in a conversation, and even how they may feel about the organization overall.

Vocal signals refer to tone of voice, pitch, volume, speed of speech, and are like body language in that they are not about what is being said but *how*. For example, think of the way interest and even attraction can be communicated much more by the tone of the voice than by the words used. Depending on the tone, volume, speed, and pitch, even a simple phrase such as "Good evening" can convey anything from "Wow, you're gorgeous" to "I'd like to get away from you as quickly as possible."

In a contact center, callers nearly always begin a call by greeting the contact center advisor before making their specific enquiry or request. When the caller customer gives a slower, lower pitched, "Good evening/morning/hello," with a slight rising or falling intonation at the end, as though asking a question, this tends to indicate interest and that the customer is prepared to invest some time—within reason—in the conversation. If the greeting is delivered in a shorter, high-pitched, clipped "Good evening/good morning," or a monotone, expressionless version, the customer is signaling that time—and interest in the organization is limited.

Once the service conversation begins, the intonation of even a single word can communicate an immense variety of emotions and meanings. For example, anyone with experience of children will be familiar with the variations in intonation of the one-word response "Yeah," and know that it can communicate anything from enthusiastic agreement, grudging acceptance, varying degrees of skepticism, to total disbelief.

If contact center agents speak in a monotone, with little variation in pitch, pace, or tone of voice, as well as sounding boring and dull, they are perceived as being bored. When this happens customers stop believing that the other person is really interested in or committed to helping them—even if what they are saying is truly caring and generous. It reinforces a cynical attitude on the part of the customer.

Equally a loud volume, a booming tone, and too much variation in pitch makes a service provider organization seem overbearing and pushy—undermining the authenticity and credibility that will impress. If advisors speak too quietly or too slowly, they can appear submissive or even depressed. Some regional accents can provide the modulation in voice pitch and pace that capture customers' interest—but it's also a skill that can be learned.

An important factor when communicating readiness to help is learning to listen for intonation. Rising or falling intonation, especially when accompanied by a drop in volume, is a "turn-yielding cue," whereby speakers signal that they have finished what they are saying and are ready to listen to the other person.

It has become fashionable to end phrases with a rising intonation but bear in mind that some customers can interpret this as indicating that it is their turn to speak. If service staff frequently end sentences on a rising or falling intonation, with a drop in volume, and then carry on without allowing the customer to speak, the customer will become frustrated and annoyed. Equally, if a service provider takes his or her turn when the customer has not given any "turn-yielding cues," even if the customer has finished a sentence, this will be seen as an interruption, and the customer will feel irritated.

Loyalty-building experience 2: "I spoke to a person who appeared/sounded positive and eager to help."

This loyalty-building experience marks the customers' perception of a significant attitude change. When customers score their perception of this experience high, it's because they have noticed the difference between a "what do you want?" type of attitude and a "how can I help?" attitude. It's a much friendlier and more personable approach.

Our research also regularly identifies the following as major customer service issues:

- failure to deliver the service being promised
- impersonal service from agents
- poorly trained agents
- not enough people to answer queries.

In fact, service providers often come in for particular criticism, with customers frequently describing them as "ignorant," "rude," "unwilling to help," and as having a lack of understanding not only of their own business but also of the needs of the customer. It's no wonder that ensuring service providers actively convince customers that they are *eager* and *willing* to help offers such an advantage in building customer loyalty.

Although a customer's initial impression depends more on appearance, body language, and voice than on what is actually said, moving on successfully to meet a customer's need or enquiry requires good conversation skills.

The art of conversation is really just a matter of knowing its conventions, the unwritten laws governing talking and listening with other people. It is a distinguishing feature of the best organizations that their customers feel they have participated in a helpful and useful conversation, rather than a "service encounter" or worse still, a transaction.

For all of us, the best and most enjoyable conversations may seem entirely spontaneous, but the people involved are still obeying rules. The difference is that they are following the rules automatically, without consciously trying, just as skilled, experienced drivers do not have to think about changing gears. But understanding how the rules of conversation work—like learning how and when to change gears—helps service providers converse more fluently and effectively.

One of the most powerful changes in the new economy is the increasing financial independence of women. An increasingly important factor in delivering this LBE to customers is appreciating how the sexes differ in their habits of talking and listening.

Learning to communicate effectively with women makes sound financial sense. But little has been done to research and adopt methods that will connect more successfully with female customers. Male preferences predominate, neglecting the fact that women view language, listening, and relationship building very differently from men.

For example in their book *Why Men Don't Listen and Women Can't Read Maps* (1998), Barbara and Allan Pease's research suggests that women have a broad range of listening sounds and habits using an average of six listening expressions in a ten-second period to reflect and then feed back the speaker's emotions. They typically use up to five tones of high- and low-pitched listening sounds—including repetition of key words, "oohs and ahs." Women often nod to show they are listening, although this nodding does not imply agreement, merely an acknowledgment of emotions or ideas. Women find it easier than men to read the meaning of what is being said through voice intonation and body language.

In contrast, men have more restricted pitch range, tending to use only three tones. Men speak in a more monotonous voice, which can appear as being uninterested even though it isn't. Men's preference when they want to show that they are listening is often to use, as Pease and Pease put it, a grunt with an occasional nod. Women, however, prefer more expressive feedback and hearing only a grunt, can often believe—and complain—that a man is not really listening.

In speech too, there are marked differences. Men have a preference for short, direct sentences with specific use of vocabulary and often a literal quality. This kind of speech is clearly good for some business interactions since it can be perceived to be authoritative and competent. Women however, often use indirect language in which they may suggest, hint, or imply what they want. Indirect speech is intended to build relationships and rapport and avoid disagreements or discord. In our experience indirect talk can appear in sales and servicing situations as, for example:

- Do you think we should sign you up for a three-month or a six-month contract?
- Wouldn't it be great if we could solve all these problems for you by integrating your account details?
- Do you feel this is right way forward for you?

However, in delivering service or selling, indirect talk of this sort may be too indirect to win business from men who find it confusing, or evidence that a woman either doesn't understand or is unenthusiastic about winning their business.

Another key difference—with important implications—in the way men and women talk and listen concerns interruptions. Men usually only interrupt each other if they are becoming annoyed, competitive, or aggressive and if interrupted they can become resentful. By contrast, women often find it hard to resist interruption, especially when a male customer is expressing interest in buying something, or conversely if a man is complaining. Interruption and conversational interplay are inbuilt female strategies for building rapport. Interrupting a male customer can have the opposite effect to that intended. Instead of building rapport, men feel ignored or even belittled.

One explanation of women's reputation as great talkers is their propensity to think aloud. The female brain is wired to make it possible to "parallel process" several conversations simultaneously. This is because speech in women is controlled by specific areas of the brain, so that even while they are talking, the rest of the brain is still available for other things. It's one of the reasons why women are so adept at multi-tasking.

The opposite however is true for men, where the rule for effective communication is keep it simple. Men's sentences tend to be shorter than women's and they are usually much more structured. Men can become uncomfortable if women talk in a way that covers several subjects simultaneously, as indeed women prefer. For women to be credible and convincing when talking to men, it's much more effective to present one clear thought at a time. For example:

> *Let's discuss what exciting options you have to meet the range of financial objectives you may be considering—extending your home, buying a new car, going on a holiday—but before we do that, there is some information that I need to collect from you.*

versus:

> *Firstly, you need to provide some basic information. After that, we can discuss all the options you may have to help you meet your plans.*

In contrast, for male service providers interacting with female customers, reticence to "think aloud," to share options, and discuss freely can be perceived as cold and unfriendly. To talk only of conclusions and actions can lead women to perceive male service providers as "pushy."

In fact, keeping it simple works most of the time. While both sexes can follow "man speak," men may switch off with what appears to be the disorganized and long-winded multi-tracking approach favored by women.

Loyalty-building experience 3: "The person I spoke to listened well to what I had to say."

Listening is often cited as by far the most important of all communications skills. It doesn't come naturally to most people, so we need to work hard at it; to stop ourselves just "jumping in" and having our say. Incidence of poor listening is an everyday occurrence—and frequently observable—in friends, colleagues, and even members of our own families. We're all guilty. You don't believe us? Then see if any—or some—of the bad habits below apply to you:

- I pretend I'm paying attention when my mind is drifting off.
- I cut people off or finish their sentences because I know what they're going to say.
- When someone is speaking to me in person or on the phone, I look around the room to see what else is happening.
- When someone talks too slowly or for too long I start doing something else.
- When someone is speaking, I plan what I will say next.
- When a person speaks too fast or uses words I don't understand, I let it go and listen only for what I do understand.

Mostly, people *don't* listen—we all tend to be more interested in announcing our own views and thoughts than really listening and understanding others. This is ironic since we all like to be listened to and understood. Even in a contact center where at least 50 percent of an agent/advisors' role is to listen, our experience suggests that consistent and effective listening is the exception rather than a rule.

A useful focus to aim for when listening to another person is to try to understand how the other person feels, and to discover what he or she wants to achieve. In business and in life good listeners have distinct advantages. In our research we have found good listeners to be significantly higher rated in organizations and more effective sales performers. But being a good listener is not just about shutting up and letting the other person talk (although this certainly helps). As we have said, good listening is essentially about giving good "feedback," giving both verbal and non-verbal signals to show that you are both paying attention and interested. Effective non-verbal feedback signals include nodding, smiling, responsive facial expressions, and leaning forwards, accompanied by general positive body language such as "open" posture and posture/gesture echo. Good verbal feedback signals include the use of expressions such as "mm-hmm," "yeah," "mmm," "ah" to show interest or agreement and to encourage the other person to continue.

Long-standing research has shown that these basic feedback signals are highly effective in winning friends and influencing people. They can even result in concrete, tangible rewards: studies have found, for example, that candidates who give this sort of feedback during job interviews are more likely to be successful than those who do not.

Another effective good-listener technique is "paraphrasing." To show that you are paying attention and interested, and to encourage the customer to tell you more, it can help if you occasionally sum up what the other person has said, as in "...so you lost your bag and your keys? How did you get home?" Furthermore, another significant benefit in paraphrasing customers' input is that it builds customers' confidence and reduces any insecurities or anxieties they may have about choosing to deal with your organization over another.

Of course, if you wish to encourage the customer to talk it's important that the question at the end of the "paraphrasing" example is an "open" question, rather than a "closed" question requiring only a yes or no response. Open questions begin with one of the following words: Who, What, When, Where, How, Why. Open questions encourage respondents to give detailed replies, providing the organization with opportunities to build further rapport, surface additional service or product needs, and provide additional advice and reassurance—all of which contribute substantially to ensuring the customer feels that he or she has been listened to.

The acclaimed author Stephen Covey in *The Seven Habits of Highly Effective People* coined the expression: "Seek first to understand, and then to be understood," which serves as a constant reminder of the need to listen to the other person before you can expect him or her to listen to you. He also says that when we are understood, we feel affirmed and validated. Effective listening nurtures a sense of deepening trust and rapport with customers for three key reasons:

1. Customers are much more inclined to trust a person who shows respect for them and for what they say.
2. Customers are much more likely to trust a person when he or she has listened carefully and helpfully to their problems.
3. The more customers trust you, the more they will share.

Loyalty-building experience 4: "I felt I had enough time and did not feel rushed."

Anyone who has ever sat through a boring meeting knows that five minutes can, under some circumstances, seem like an hour. Anyone who has ever pressed a snooze button will tell you the reverse is true. Both are examples of how we experience time.

Philosophers have long argued about the nature of time. Since the early 1800s, psychologists have been testing how humans interpret the passing or duration of time. Many modern experiments rely on the theory that the cerebral cortex is the part of the brain responsible for keeping track of time and research has shown that people with damaged cerebral cortexes have difficulty in this. In experiments psychologists typically ask participants to estimate the amount of time they spend completing an activity and then change different aspects of the activity, such as its difficulty, to look for correspondence between variable aspects and the time estimates. In these experiments, the difficulty level of the activities is changed to require greater use of the cerebral cortex. Hypothetically, as the difficulty increases, less brainpower is available to keep track of time, and therefore participants would be more likely to underestimate the duration of time passing during the activity.

But a problem arises when conducting experiments involving the cerebral cortex. Imagine you are given the instruction, "Don't think about cream cakes." Chances are you'll now be thinking about cream cakes (chocolate éclairs, in our case). This phenomenon is one of the difficulties of the cerebral cortex-based experiments. If participants are told before the experiment that they are going to make time estimates, then these participants may think about time, and use more of the cerebral cortex for time-keeping than they otherwise would. To deal with this problem, psychologists differentiate between two kinds of time estimates, prospective and retrospective. In prospective time estimates, participants know beforehand that they are going to be asked to estimate time. In retrospective time estimates, participants do not know that they will be asked to estimate time at the end of the activity.

In 1990, in his book *About Time*, William Friedman published a review of 70 time experiments, which describe six ways that the duration of time is subjectively distorted. The first of the Friedman phenomena is that people underestimate time while completing attention-demanding tasks. Most experimental research shows that this phenomenon occurs because people's attention is diverted from time-keeping when they are engaged in challenging activities, in other words, time flies when you're busy. Friedman also points out however, that time slows down during periods of high expectation, nervousness, fear, or anticipation.

Further, memory can affect how you perceive time. Friedman states that a time period seems longer if remembered in detail, and shorter if remembered only in outline. Similarly, many events during a time period lead to overestimates of duration. Friedman relates these phenomena to people's tendency to assume that it takes longer for many events to occur than for a few to occur. Last, Friedman also states something we all know intuitively and from experience—that time goes by more quickly as you age. This is because the relationship between age and time perception is logarithmic, meaning that people measure time relative to their age.

For an organization to deliver this particular LBE successfully, it's vital that its staff recognize whether a customer is in a rush or in the mood for a more relaxed or leisurely interaction. "The permanent hurry" for many customers (this trend was discussed in Chapter 3) means that for customers, unless they are able to understand something quickly and easily it will often be ignored, especially if the personal relevance is not immediately clear. Today's time starvation leads to a poverty of attention, and it is quite a challenge to create an experience in which a customer perceives he or she has been given enough time—given that this will vary from individual to individual.

The secret of success is for customers to feel that time spent in a service interaction has been effectively and efficiently invested. For customers in a more relaxed mood, individualized rapport building is the measure of effectiveness—"They were interested in serving me," "I didn't feel rushed." Customers in a "permanent hurry" already feel rushed and should feel that their needs have been met along with the perception that a minimal amount of time has been invested. The value of the time spent—in terms of experience and outcome—must exceed its duration.

In this context Friedman's findings contain important lessons for delivering service experiences that will impress. Let's examine their implications in detail:

- **Engaging the customer will make time pass more quickly.** Expert neurological evidence suggests that there's a disparity in our thought processes—the mind is only conscious of a thought or decision a moment after it's made. The slower the transition between these two moments, the slower time seems to be passing. The speed of the process is dependent upon outside factors. When one is engaged, say, in an interesting conversation or task the process goes faster, making time seem to go quickly. When the transition from unconscious to conscious thought slows—during a call transfer, for example, or if a service provider is looking up details on a system—so, too, does one's perception of time. For example—"dead air" (long silences) in a phone call slows time and increases perception of inefficiencies. The best service providers fill it by talking about how products, services, or processes are relevant to the customer.

- **More events lengthen the perception of duration.** A significant frustration for many customers is the failure of many organizations to provide a single point of contact. One-to-one service remains top of many customers' priority lists when it comes to making general enquiries about their household bills or bank details. Around 94 percent of people who regularly use contact centers, for example, see their benefit as being one point of entry to a multitude of linked services: "The whole concept of a call center is to provide access to multi services. I want to be able to dial a number and be able to access the entire organization's customer service via this one point of contact." Technology combined with more effective training to create multiskilled organizations is the key to future success.

- **A given interval seems longer if a judgment of the duration is anticipated.** Because of the "permanent hurry," it is natural to assume that telling customers "this will only take a couple of minutes" will please them. But it is important to avoid this at all costs. This phrase triggers the cerebral cortex to focus on time passing, with the result that the customers will subsequently over-estimate the duration of the interaction. In order to impress hurried customers, it's far more effective to refer to time passing *after* a task has been completed. "That only took a couple of minutes" is much more likely to leave customers feeling that time has been efficiently used.

- **A duration seems longer if we are frustrated, waiting for a positive experience, or waiting for a specific event.**

- **An interval seems longer if it is remembered in more detailed pieces and shorter if we think of it more simply.** When it comes to dealing with hurried customers, many contact center agents believe that these customers want to end a call as quickly as possible. In our research however, we find this to be a mistake—for two reasons.

First, the research suggests that memory affects our perception of how time passes—when we remember more detailed interactions, we believe that they have taken longer to resolve, even though this is not necessarily the case. The best agents in contact centers we've worked with often summarize the actions they have taken on a customers' behalf at the end of a call. The summary fools the customer's memory of the interaction into simpler chunks—creating the impression that less time has been taken.

Second, in the rush to deal with the call, there is always the danger of failing to deal with the customer's whole query or concern; this problem is known as "failure demand." It was discussed in Chapter 4, in which the seriously adverse financial implications of it were addressed in detail.

At Egnatia Bank, the customer service experience has been considerably enhanced with the use of speech-enabled interactive voice recognition (IVR), with initial estimates of take-up rate (15 percent of call volumes) being considerably exceeded. Speech-enabled IVR puts the customer in control of the time they invest, and frees agents from routine transactions to focus on more complex requests from customers, and very likely also more profitable ones.

Loyalty-building experience 5: "I got a chance to ask any questions I had."

Our research has shown that when customers have formulated questions about a product or service, they *feel* smarter and better informed, which are key elements in feeding self-esteem. The emotional response is almost independent of whether the questions are satisfactorily answered—though rationally this is clearly important too. An "accelerator" is to create a space for customers to ask a question; the "inhibitor" is not to give them time to think of one.

Success in generating this particular LBE depends on a service provider's ability to engage customers in the encounter. Customers feel better about their decisions if they have asked a relevant and credible question: "How will that benefit me?", "What options do I have?" It also provides an excellent opportunity for a service provider to offer customers reassurance and potentially additional service. The secret lies in creating the opportunity for customers to think of how the product or service will bring them individual benefit.

Setting up this opportunity is a sophisticated skill that also involves the use of questions. Good questions invite customers to convey what they are thinking and to talk through their decision-making processes and concerns.

Another important aspect of questioning is waiting for customers to respond. Our research indicates that the average time we wait for responses is less than three seconds, and service providers should allow for more time for customers to think through their responses.

Probing questions are an assessment strategy that provides insight into the mental processes a customer is using by engaging him or her in conversation about the subject. The goal of the questions is to deepen the customers' knowledge and subsequently boost their self-esteem.

Sample probing questions

- How did you know that?
- What factors did you use to decide?
- Can you show us how you did that?
- Can that be done another way?
- What if I changed [some element of problem]?

If customers do not get the opportunity to think about potential questions at the time of the service interaction, there are at least two potential consequences. First, a query or need goes unmet, which undermines the ability of the organization to impress. Second, customers seeking clarification or further service and attention, will, if you're lucky, return to give the organization another chance at resolution or they may go elsewhere. Neither outcome is desirable.

At a more pragmatic level, another important element is ensuring that service providers understand the etiquette of conversational turn-taking. For instance, how many of us have ever felt bombarded by a service provider that has got into his or her stride so that the conversation has felt like either a steamroller or a roller-coaster? Contact center agents in particular, are taught to how to *control a call*—in order to manage call-handling times. The downside is that many contact centers suffer from up to 30 percent on average in "failure demand," which is the measure of customers calling back because a service need was not resolved at first contact.

Once a service conversation is underway, a successful outcome—that is, customers who feel so impressed with the service that they rate the experience as "ten out of ten" will depend as much on interpersonal skills as product or process knowledge.

We have probably all encountered at least one person in our lives who is highly articulate, witty, and amusing, but who loses friends and alienates people by hogging the conversation, not allowing others to get a word in edgeways. In life, there is the equally irritating strong, silent type who never asks a question, or never expresses interest. While these people don't last long in service jobs, they may still be customers who'll need to be engaged in a service encounter in order to feel impressed.

In the service environment, it may be that what we have to say to customers is fascinating, and we may express it with great eloquence, but if we've not grasped the basic social skills involved in conversational turn-taking, we'll be perceived as arrogant and unpleasant. Customers will not enjoy dealing with us and nor, for that matter, will anyone else.

A basic rule on how much to talk is very simple: contributions in terms of air-time to the conversation should be roughly equal. The essence of a good conversation is reciprocity: give-and-take, sharing, and exchange, with both parties contributing equally as talkers and as listeners.

Achieving this balance depends on knowing when to take our turn in a conversation, as well as when and how to "yield the floor." So, how do we know when it is our turn to speak? Pauses are not necessarily an infallible guide—one study found that the length of the average pause during speech was 0.807 seconds, while the average pause between speakers was shorter, only 0.764 seconds. In other words, people clearly use signals other than pauses to indicate that they have finished speaking.

In previous sections, we have described in detail the various non-verbal signals people use to show that they have finished what they are saying, and that it is another person's turn to speak. These also include eye-contact signals (remember that people look away more when they are speaking, so when they look back, this often indicates that it is your turn) and vocal signals such as rising or falling intonation, with a drop in volume. This may be accompanied by verbal "turn-yielding" signals, such as the completion of a clause or "tailing off" into meaningless expressions such as "you know."

As a general rule, the more of these turn-yielding cues that occur simultaneously, the more likely it is that the other person has finished and expects you to speak. Watching and/or listening for these clues will help avoid interrupting, and also awkward gaps and lengthy pauses in the conversation.

Loyalty-building experience 6: "The person I spoke to seemed to have a good knowledge of what he/she was talking about."

Over the last ten years, in the many thousands of customer focus groups, discussions, and interviews that we've conducted, customers always cite well trained, knowledgeable and even "expert" staff among the top three on their wish list for ideal organizations. This is a consequence of the "trust implosion," and something that causes a great many customers to worry.

But how would a customer really know if a member of an organization did not know what he or she was talking about, until it was too late? What signals can organizations give to reassure customers that they can be trusted to take care of them? There are a number of interwoven factors.

In their engaging book, *The Soul of The New Consumer* (2001), David Lewis and Daniel Bridger show how people are motivated to purchase or experience products and services that they like and perceive as authentic. They conduct a number of experiments to explore the relationship between liking and authenticity. In one such experiment they describe how customers were asked to rate their liking for a small green glass bottle on a scale from 1 (not at all) to 5 (a great deal). Some customers were told nothing about the history of the bottle while others were told it had been discovered in the ruins of Pompeii, the ancient city buried by the eruption of Mount Vesuvius in AD 79.

Lewis and Bridger found that those who believed that they were holding an authentic relic from the catastrophe rated their liking significantly higher than those who were given no information about the bottle. This suggests that, as a general rule, when we perceive something to be authentic we are more likely to like it.

In another part of the experiment they found that liking an object also conferred upon it the property of authenticity. Lewis and Bridger asked customers to rate their liking for a small, barnacle-encrusted figurine. They were then told that it was believed to come from *Titanic* and asked to rate the degree to which they considered this to be true. Those who liked the object were more inclined to believe it had come from *Titanic* than those who disliked it.

The finding that liking and authenticity are interlinked is borne out in research that well-liked brands—such as Disney, Virgin, and Apple—are considered to offer highly authentic products and experiences.

When it comes to convincing customers that an organization is trustworthy, however, credibility is a more practical focus than authenticity for individual organizations.

A credible source of information makes for quicker and firmer decisions. A credible person is expert (experienced, qualified, intelligent, skilled) and trustworthy (honest, fair, unselfish, caring). Credibility is context-dependent, and an expert in one situation may be incompetent in another. Actions that enhance credibility include:

- highlighting individual experience and qualifications
- showing you care about the other person and have his or her best interests at heart
- showing you are similar to the other person by using his or her language, pace of speech, mannerisms, and so on
- being assertive; quickly and logically refuting counter-arguments
- highlighting the credibility of your organization.

Language that reduces credibility includes:

- Ums, ers, and other, ah, hesitation.
- Excessive exaggeration.
- Vague kinds of qualifications that sort of lack assertion.
- Excessive politeness that indicates subordination.
- Most importantly of all, a key factor in enhancing credibility is to leverage the credibility of others by getting introduced by a credible person. There is no higher form of credibility than word of mouth and personal recommendation.

Loyalty-building experience 7: "The person I spoke to at the organization really gave me the impression that he/she enjoyed speaking to me."

This LBE is linked to the relationship between liking, authenticity, and credibility. It turns the tables on whether the organization is liked to show the importance of the customer feeling that a service provider has been motivated by, or even *enjoyed* providing service. The encounter may have been face to face or by phone, and its importance in bridging to a further encounter or reinforcing a lasting good impression is vital.

Winning this endorsement from customers is largely based on the skill of rapport building. Rapport building is about charming or in some sense "chatting up" a customer. Whenever we make this recommendation to clients, many of the less experienced organizations seem to be obsessed with the issue of how to go about this—in particular what their opening line should be.

But what comes as a big shock to many of our clients is the fact that frequently—indeed, at least half of the time—it is the *customer* who uses a positive, constructive, and "chatty" opening line that could be the basis of a positive and constructive interaction, but that the customer service staff member then "blanks" the customer and spoils the rapport. The staff member may not be sufficiently interested in creating a rapport (which raises the question of why he or she is doing that job *at all*), or the staff member may be laboring under thoughtless training or management practice that has focused unduly on maximizing call-handling volume, or sales.

This "blanking" of a customer's opening line is a huge inhibitor of this particular loyalty-inspiring feeling. If it happens the customer often feels stupid and unappreciated and will withdraw emotionally from the encounter as quickly as possible in order to "save face." While this may inadvertently help meet time management targets, it won't help sales or customer retention figures.

To help service providers begin rapport-building conversations more effectively, but also recognize when rapport building is customer initiated, let's look at "openers" in more detail. Interestingly, the choice of opening line is not really very important, and striving for originality and wit is a wasted effort. The fact is that conversational "openers" are rarely original, witty, or elegant, and here's the newsflash, *no one expects them to be*. The best openers are, quite simply, those that can easily be recognized as openers—as attempts to start a conversation. In the United Kingdom, the traditional comment on the weather, for example ("Nice day, isn't it?" or "Doesn't feel much like summer, eh?") will do just fine, as everyone knows that it is a conversation starter. The fact that these comments are phrased as questions, or with a rising "interrogative" intonation, does not mean that the speaker is unsure about the quality of the weather and requires confirmation: it means that the speaker is inviting a response in order to start a conversation. In the United Kingdom, it is universally understood that such weather comments have nothing to do with the weather, and they are universally accepted as conversation starters. Saying "Lovely day, isn't it?" (or a rainy-day equivalent) is the UK way of saying "I'd like to talk to you; will you talk to me?"

A friendly response, including positive body language, means, "Yes, I'll talk to you"; a monosyllabic or monotone response (possibly accompanied by body language) often signals lack of time and means, "No, I don't have time for this." The words chosen to open a conversation aimed at rapport building are really quite unimportant, and there is no point in striving to be witty or amusing. Much more important is the tone of voice. To effectively open a rapport-building opportunity, it's sufficient to make a vague, impersonal comment, either phrased as a question or with a rising intonation as though asking a question.

This formula—the impersonal interrogative comment—has evolved as the standard method of initiating conversation with strangers because it is extremely effective. The non-personal nature of the comment makes it unthreatening and non-intrusive; the interrogative (questioning) tone or "isn't it?" ending invites a response, but is not as demanding as a direct or open question.

There is a big difference between an interrogative comment such as "Cold today, isn't it?" and a direct and open question such as "What do you think of this weather?" This direct question demands and requires a reply, while the interrogative comment allows the other person some flexibility. He or she may decide to respond minimally, expansively, or not at all, if he or she does not wish to invest in developing rapport.

There are, of course, degrees of positive and negative response to an impersonal interrogative comment. The significant factors are length, personalizing, and questioning. In gauging the willingness of the customer to participate in rapport-building conversation, the longer the response, the better. If the customer responds to your comment with a reply of the same length or longer, this is a good sign. A personalized response, that is, one including the word "I" (as in, for example, "Yes, I love this weather"), is even more positive. A personalized response ending in a question or interrogative (rising) intonation (as in "I thought it was supposed to clear up by this afternoon?") is even better, and a personalized response involving a personalized question, that is, a response including the words "I" and "you," is the most positive of all. So, if you say, "Nice day, isn't it?" and the customer replies, "Yes, I was getting so tired of all that rain, weren't you?" you are definitely developing a deeper level of rapport.

What is really interesting here is that there's nothing original, witty, or clever about the above exchange. It could even be dismissed as polite, boring, and insignificant. But in fact, a great deal of vital information has been exchanged. The opener has been recognized as a friendly invitation to a conversation, the invitation has been accepted, the customer has revealed something about him/herself, expressed interest in talking with you, and even suggested that you might have something in common. Remember, the opening remark in a rapport-building conversation may often come from the customer—so build on it!

Another factor that concerns many of the organizations that we have met over the years is the use of humor. Humor is perhaps the most powerful relationship-building tool, yet it can easily backfire if abused or misused.

On the positive side, studies have shown that people who use humor are perceived as more likeable, and that both trust and attraction increase when a light-hearted approach is used. Judicious use of humor can reduce anxiety and establish a relaxed mood that helps a relationship to develop more rapidly. On the negative side, inappropriate use of humor can kill a promising relationship stone dead in a matter of seconds.

While it is clearly important to avoid causing offence, humor, used at the right time, conveys the sense that we are liked and appreciated. Liking something or someone, as we have discussed, also has the effect of enhancing credibility and authenticity. As humans we have a natural instinct to make people we like smile; shared smiles and laughter provide reassurance.

The most common mistakes in use of humor involve its over-use or under-use. As a general rule, men are more likely to over-use humor, while women sometimes have a tendency to under-use humor—and to adopt a too serious tone when a more light-hearted banter would be more effective.

Failing to respond in kind (if appropriate) to a customer's use of humor can make the customer feel he or she isn't liked, which is undermining to self-esteem.

Another, deeper, form of rapport building is reciprocal disclosure. This technique is used by the most successful service providers, and involves the exchange of personal information. Reciprocal disclosure creates a deeper rapport because it conveys intimacy, even if the exchange of information is nothing more intimate than sharing a liking for warm weather, caravan holidays, or hotdogs.

If a customer discloses some such detail, the best service providers recognize the opportunity to reciprocate as soon as possible by revealing some similar information about themselves. By offering slightly more personal information, it is possible to assess the effectiveness of the technique in building deep rapport. If the customer likes you, he or she will probably try to "match" your disclosure with one of similar value. Reciprocal disclosure of this kind is much more subtle and less threatening than asking direct personal questions.

A critical success factor is to always maintain a balance in disclosures between customer and staff member. If a service provider gets too far ahead by revealing too much—the customer will perceive a credibility gap or if the service provider is lagging behind by revealing too little, the customer will feel rebuffed.

Loyalty-building experience 8: "The interaction was concluded to my complete satisfaction."

Every salesperson knows that there is little point in establishing a great rapport with customers, attracting their interest, gaining their trust and so on, if you fail to "close" (sales-speak for actually making the sale, securing the contract, getting the customer to hand over money, or sign on the dotted line).

Amazing as it may seem, many of the organizations we have met over the last ten years still do not accept the basic fact that if a customer has been impressed by a service encounter, he or she will end up wanting more—which equals more service and more sales.

Conclusion

There is a fascinating, if obscure, aspect to modern-day complexity theory known as "the law of requisite variety." This law states that to control a system, the controlling unit must have more options and choices in its responses than the system it is attempting to control. In human systems, the idea translates into the principle that the person with the greatest flexibility of behavior—that is, the greatest number of ways of interacting—will control the system. When service providers are able to vary their behavior, they are more likely to get the desired outcome—that is, for customers to feel impressed.

Increasing awareness of the LBEs and the tools that support them correspondingly increases the flexibility of the behavior of customer service staff, increasing their effectiveness. Organizations need to take on board without delay the lesson that if what they are doing now is not working as far as generating loyalty from impressed customers is concerned, then the organization needs to do something radical about it—and urgently. After all, almost anything is better than continuing with what doesn't work.

For organizations today, what matters is winning customer loyalty from customers who will become so loyal that they will in effect want to sell and promote the organization themselves. Everything else is, in a very real sense, just conversation.

8 Making loyalty-building experiences happen

For any organization, knowing about the importance of the eight incremental stages of loyalty-building experiences (LBEs) is of great importance if it is do justice to its potential for winning customer loyalty. But being aware of these eight incremental stages of creating a glorious totality of an irresistible loyalty-winning interaction is only the start; what really matters is putting them into practice. In this chapter, we look at the process of doing so, and how it works at the coalface of an organization's interactions with its customers.

We profile our own activities in doing this because these are the activities we know best. In any case, the concept of the LBE is one we have developed at Cape Consulting, and is an original concept that is not put into practice anywhere else. It is also proprietary to our firm.

Our experience at Cape Consulting is that there are four preliminary issues that must be addressed to create an environment in which LBEs can be put into practice successfully. These four preliminary issues are as follows:

1. Facing up to the challenge

The most momentous journey does indeed begin with just one step. If you want to make the most of the transformation potential of LBEs for your organization, the first step to take involves accepting the nature of the challenge with which you need to engage.

Let's be very clear about the nature of this challenge. You are not going to set your sights anywhere near as low as the aim of changing a "bad" caliber of customer service to "good." No—if you aren't already starting out on this journey with an organization that is *already* offering "good" customer service, then you had better up the ante of your customer service before you start thinking about how to use LBEs. For, strictly speaking, the purpose of identifying and isolating LBEs as a concept and practical reality is not to facilitate the creation of merely good service, but rather to help an organization move the quality of its service from being good to becoming "great."

For every customer, every time.

2. Creating clarity

If you have read this far in this book, you will be unlikely to have much doubt that all organizations need to maximize the extent and quality of customer recommendations, and that this requirement is especially important for any organization selling service brands.

Our work and research at Cape Consulting is based around careful monitoring and measurement of LBEs at specific organizations, and the development of specific initiatives to help a client organization implement LBEs more successfully. In other words, clarity must be created about what needs to be done to implement LBEs.

This initial work involves, above all, listening to the organization's staff dealing with customers, and researching customers' perception of their experiences. Subsequently, diagnostic information is shared with the management team to develop a practical plan and method to improve the delivery of LBEs by staff interacting with customers.

3. Creating "climate"

In practice, developing team managers so that they can create the "climate" for the LBEs to be delivered is an essential step in the transformation of the quality of an organization's service from "good" to "great."

The way this development of team managers usually works is by events being held which focus on equipping team managers to support the delivery of LBEs through:

- developing team managers to be able to coach team members in the required practices
- customizing our generic LBE-measuring tool to prioritize specific and practical actions for advisers to deliver during every interaction with every customer.

4. Creating consistency

Our work in the area of helping client organizations transform the quality of their customer service is focused on enabling clients to win new—and on occasion previously undreamt-of—levels of customer loyalty. In practical terms, the work involves developing customer service staff, team managers, technical advisers, and telephony coaches to radically improve customer experiences.

Above all, our work involves:

- communicating the nature of LBEs to everyone at the client organization who will be involved with the initiative to improve customers experiences
- implementing our LBE measurement tool.

In this way, the LBEs create consistency and give customer service staff clarity about what they must do to maximize the opportunity to create a recommending customer—for every customer, every time.

Now let's look at how one particular organization focused on LBEs and put them into practice in one of its major customer contact centers. The organization is Norwich Union Insurance, and we are grateful to our client John Willmott, director of organizational change at Norwich Union Insurance, for providing us with this account of how his organization is implementing an original new technique to cause a paradigm shift in the quality of customer service it offers via its customer contact centers.

John Willmott, Norwich Union Insurance

In the enormously competitive retail financial services markets of today, being good enough is no longer good enough.

At Norwich Union Insurance we have always believed—I hope justifiably—that we offer a high level of customer service from our customer contact centers. But this is no longer enough for our customers, for our partners, or for ourselves. We want to offer a quality of service that is really special; a level of service which, if we can get it right, might even be great.

With 13 000 employees and total annual premiums of almost £8 billion, Norwich Union Insurance, the general insurance arm of Aviva plc, is the UK's largest insurer. We provide 60 percent of Aviva's worldwide general insurance business by gross written premium. In 2004 Norwich Union generated an operating profit of £832 million. Altogether we operate 15 customer contact centers in the UK and three in India. These employ a total of 8000 people.

Our commercial landscape is ever more competitive; our customers ever more demanding. To survive and prosper, we must embrace radical change. We must reduce our costs of doing business and we must improve customer service. Our fundamental perception—and the implications of this point are massive and ongoing—is that a traditional, "ordinary" level of contact center performance will not deliver the differentiated, exceptional caliber of customer service that wins enthusiastic loyalty from customers.

A major part of what Norwich Union does involves selling insurance to customers directly. But like most large insurance companies and many other types of financial services organization, we also place a major emphasis on developing relationships with third-party organizations to furnish them with a variety of services. These services include being, in effect, the partners' own customer contact center.

My job as director of customer service for our partners is to ensure that their own customers do indeed enjoy a level of service that is much better than merely "good."

Norwich Union began working with partners in the 1970s. This was comparatively recently in our 200-year history, yet we were in fact one of the first insurers to start getting involved with this area of business. From the moment we initiated this new revenue stream we have regarded our ability to offer a top-notch service to partners and their own customers to be an essential part of our corporate strategy and competitive differentiation. Today, the business we have with our partners is worth a quarter of our annual turnover.

The precise nature of the processes we carry out for our partners varies according to their particular requirements.

In some cases we take on the complete responsibility for a partner's insurance offering and deliver that offering essentially as a turn-key service. When this happens, our staff deal with the partner's customers' insurance requirement from start to finish—that is, from sales to claims resolution—as though we were the partner's own staff.

Other partners, especially those with strong, high-profile brands, may prefer to retain control of their sales and branding but will make use of our own people in administering and managing the insurance product, again including handling claims. In practice, this second type of arrangement tends to be the most popular with partners.

Ideally, both types of arrangement give our partners' customers the peace of mind, security and square deal they associate with a brand they know and trust—the partner's brand. The partner's customers also benefit from the long-term expertise, strong capitalization and reliability of the Norwich Union.

But whether we are offering a partner an entire turn-key service, or focusing on the administration and management of the insurance product, including claims handling, the entire arrangement cannot possibly be a successful one for the three parties concerned—the customer, the partner, and ourselves—unless the quality of service we provide to the partner's customer is absolutely top-notch.

In my professional life, I adhere rigorously to the creed that in the financial services industry, as in other major sectors, product pricing is a crucial factor in winning customers. But if you really want to keep customers, what really matters is the quality of customer service you extend to them.

Following on logically from the implications of this creed, we decided to take vigorous steps to investigate what we could do to make the quality of the service we offer to our partners' customers even better than we believed it already was.

Research into the theory of customer loyalty

A sensible first step seemed to be to find a consultancy that had in-depth experience in the customer service and customer loyalty arenas and could give us advice about practical steps we could put into practice to achieve our aim. As a result of our research, we made contact with an organization that had already been in touch with us: the service excellence consultancy, Cape Consulting.

The first advice we were given by Cape Consulting was that we ought to familiarize ourselves with the work of the business thinker Frederick Reichheld, author of the best-selling book *The Loyalty Effect* and its sister publication *Loyalty Rules*.

I found reading Reichheld an invigorating and inspiring experience. In these two books, Reichheld is unequivocal in his belief that customer loyalty, far from merely being a subset of what a business should all be about, is—in fact—the *totality* of what a business's focus should be.

What I found particularly interesting about Reichheld's work is that he has ingeniously reduced his thinking about customer loyalty to proposing that the best and most reliable test of this should simply consist of the customer's response to the question, would you recommend this organization to a friend?

Indeed, Reichheld has drilled down even farther into the subject. He has actually developed ways of measuring customers' willingness to recommend on a scale of between zero and ten.

Reichheld has modeled the results against organizations' sales growth and shown that when there are significantly more *promoters* (that is, enthusiastic recommenders of the organization in question) than there are *detractors* (that is, those scoring comparatively low on the recommendation scale), then it is likely that sales growth among these loyalty leaders will substantially exceed growth among competitors who do not have significantly more promoters than detractors.

The terms "promoters" and "detractors," by the way, are Reichheld's invention. They seem appropriate for the exposition of his basic thesis, which is that anything less than an enthusiastic willingness to recommend makes someone essentially a detractor.

This is a crucially important point. In Reichheld's world there are no "A"s for effort when it comes to inducing someone to be *almost* willing to recommend an organization. Only success in winning their enthusiastic willingness to recommend counts.

After steeping ourselves in Reichheld's ideas, and then holding further discussions with Cape Consulting, we decided that if we wanted to effect a major improvement beyond merely being "good" in the quality of the customer service we offered our partners' customers, we would need to define and pursue a clear and decisive course of action. Above all, we would need to do everything we could to improve the quality of the customer service experience our partners' customers were receiving from our customer contact centers.

The challenge that faced us

The substance of the challenge that confronted us was that, as I've suggested above, we knew our customer service was pretty good already. We weren't, therefore, in a situation where we had to dismantle everything we were already doing and start again. From some perspectives that might have been easier than what we actually had to achieve, which was to raise a system that was already performing well another rung—or preferably even several rungs—up the ladder of quality.

When an organization already believes itself to be good in some particular respect, there is a huge challenge involved in overcoming the inertia of the status quo. People see no compelling reason to change what is already working perfectly well. Their creed tends to be that rather over-used but nonetheless commonsense mantra, "if it isn't broken, don't fix it."

But we were confident the way ahead we had chosen was the right one. And so, starting with our call center in Bishopbriggs—a suburb of Glasgow—we began working closely with our call center agents to develop an entirely new mindset as far as dealing with customers was concerned.

Our initial research

We decided to appoint Cape Consulting to assist us with this initiative. Our work with Cape Consulting began with a programme of customer research in which we measured our ability to generate enthusiastic customers who would be "promoters" according to Reichheld's terminology. We then modeled our ability in this direction against Cape Consulting's database of loyalty-building experiences (LBEs). The term was developed by Cape Consulting itself. LBEs can be defined as experiences that result in a customer feeling more loyal to an organization.

LBEs indicate that a customer is enjoying, and feeling comfortable about, his interaction with the organization.

In particular, LBEs are designed to investigate that the customer feels that:

- he or she has sufficient time to think, without feeling rushed
- he or she is appreciated as an individual
- dealing with the organization is easy, convenient, efficient and enjoyable
- the organization genuinely cares about meeting his or her needs
- he or she is getting a really good deal from the organization.

Putting the research into action

In business good research is always important, but devising and implementing applications that literally capitalize on the research and win competitive advantage from it is what really matters. We aligned Cape Consulting's LBEs to a programme we already had underway to improve the quality of customer service experiences. That programme had defined the ends. Cape Consulting's work defined the means. We named our new programme "Care at the Heart."

The idea behind the "Care at the Heart" programme was that we would very consciously set specific objectives for how our customers would feel when they dealt with us. We then identified what changes we could make in how we communicated with our customers, to give them the feelings we wanted them to have. This objective—giving customers those feelings—was the key aspect of the procedure.

Achieving this objective required a vigorous programme of decisive action. Like many in the call center industry, I believe that the biggest influence on the performance of call center agents is their team leader. And so we created a programme that involved team leaders *teaching* their teams how to achieve the LBEs that we had, very literally, set at the heart of the Care at the Heart programme.

We were delighted to find that the LBEs gave the programme an unprecedented level of credibility among call center agents and team leaders. In particular, the enthusiasm of team leaders was infectious—in the best sense of the word—and their teams benefited enormously from it.

The practical intervention

What was the particular nature of the intervention at the actual "coal-face" where call center agents deal with customers on the phone?

Above all, the telephone interaction between the call center agent and the customer became guided by specific target behaviors that the agents were encouraged to put into action in a natural and—above all—*authentic* fashion.

The reasons why authenticity has been the key to the programme's success are:

- A lack of authenticity is easy to detect in voice, tone and manner.
- A commitment to offer really excellent service is often called "emotional labor." An agent must want to deliver the LBEs. If he or she doesn't, no sustained improvements are going to happen.
- If agents don't enjoy the experience of talking to customers, their jobs can be very mundane indeed. A principal purpose of the programme is to help call center agents realize that their jobs will actually become more interesting and more enjoyable if they put these practices into action.

Making progress

Overall, the work itself consisted of three key phases: a diagnostic phase, an implementation phase and a "business as usual" phase.

The diagnostic phase posed the following key questions:

- Do we impress our customers through their service experiences?
- Do our people know how to impress customers?
- Are we supporting a contact center environment where our agents are given the opportunity to perform to a high level?
- How can we support our front-line managers in driving improvements to customer experiences?

Cape Consulting's diagnostic processes involved a range of tools: quantitative assessment of customers' service experience and the identification of Reichheld's all-important scores to identify performance gaps that had to be closed, and thereby increase the likelihood of creating promoters.

Cape Consulting assessed calls between our contact center through call listening. Our performance climate was measured, relative to Cape Consulting's existing database, on such key dimensions as:

- strategic clarity
- performance standards
- teamwork
- recognition and motivation
- responsibility and commitment.

It's important to point out that because we know our Team Manager population to be ultimately the most influential factor of all affecting the performance of our customer contact center staff, Cape Consulting used an audit of coaching skills and practices to make recommendations to increase the effectiveness of this important group.

The implementation phase involved team managers becoming even more involved at the heart of the process. They ran events for their teams that shared customers' feedback and data. This allowed team managers to communicate to their call center agents important discoveries about the agents' current level of performance. Contact center staff were shown that while certainly they were good at what they did, there were many areas where they could potentially make improvements.

Finally, there was the "business as usual" phase in which we in effect "rebooted" our activities to include the new working practices we had developed that incorporated the major new emphasis on achieving the LBEs.

These new working practices, and the feedback processes that were a crucial element of them, were essential to our key task of instilling new behaviors. Again, the difference was between knowing what to do and actually doing it. We have found that implementation has taken dogged effort and persistence to convert those contact center staff that were still comfortably doing just enough to satisfy customers but not enough to impress them.

Conclusion

The Care at the Heart programme is still continuing. I think it is fair to say that it has allowed us at Norwich Union to achieve a paradigm shift in how call center agents do their job. Making this paradigm shift happen has been a major undertaking and one that still needs constant vigilance. People do not change their behavior overnight; they have to be repeatedly persuaded to change it, and given positive reasons to want to change it.

It is true that some aspects of Cape's intervention did involve scripting the new way of dealing with customers. And because the call center agents were dealing with financial services, there were some necessary regulatory and technical aspects of the conversation that had to be included.

But the general approach has not been to inflict scripts on our agents but rather to create a collaborative atmosphere within call center agent teams where individual agents feel motivated to work together in the team to collaborate on achieving an enormous change for the better in how they deal with customers.

The response to the initiative from individual call center agents at Bishopbriggs has been extremely inspiring and encouraging. Many people who work in call centers are young people starting what is often their first job. Labor mobility within call centers is quite high, and in the past many agents have taken it for granted that their work would be rather boring and not very "human." We have shown, I think, that this does not need to be the case.

The hard facts are there too. Sales are up. The virulent problem of "failure demand"—when customers have to make a second call to clarify some problem that was not dealt with properly the first time round—is down. Motivation is up. Our net promoter scores are up across the board.

I have no doubt at all that we can differentiate our products and services from those of our rivals by striving to offer a better level of customer service than they do. And for us, this enhanced customer service is won by focusing very carefully, thoughtfully and creatively on how the agents in our customer contact centers actually talk to customers—and the authenticity and care with which these agents respond to customers' needs.

9   The future

In the early years of the nineteenth century, clerks at the branch of the Martins Bank in Liverpool (England) would habitually add, as an additional security measure, short descriptions of customers in the bank's signature book. One rather unflattering entry described a female customer as a "little pug-faced woman with a squeaky voice."

No one is likely to enjoy the idea of being described as being pug-faced and having a squeaky voice, or indeed knowing that any similarly unflattering description of them is held on a bank's internal ledgers. Still, the unfortunate lady whose physiognomy and vocal charms were recorded for the bank's employees, and for posterity, can rest in her grave knowing that she was at least given a significant element of personal recognition by the nameless bankers who wrote down what she looked like.

This book, *Customer Loyalty: a guide for time travelers*, has essentially been a hymn in praise of organizations that take the trouble to get to know their customers on an individual basis and offer them a personal level of service that truly impresses them.

Our first core belief in this book has been our conviction that intrinsically customers want to be loyal. They enjoy finding an organization to which they can be loyal and they are likely to regard the organization that wins their loyalty with the same level of excitement and affection with which they regard their friends.

We've focused on the notion of time travel because of our second fundamental belief, which is that in order to give customers what they want it's necessary to take the trouble to understand the social factors and social trends affecting customer behavior and desires. This means that the organization has to be sensitive to changing trends over time. In other words, the organization has to become something of a time traveler.

A recent convention in the United States organized by time travel enthusiasts was deliberately geared to inviting people from the future in the hope that some time travelers from the future might indeed turn up. Unfortunately, but perhaps not entirely surprisingly, there was no record of any futuristic people appearing at the convention in a suitably glamorous time machine. But if people may not be able to return to the present from the future, we can at least look into the future from our current perspective and speculate. What kind of developments do customer loyalty professionals need to anticipate as we move into the future at our pedestrian but inexorable pace of 60 minutes an hour, 24 hours per day?

While this book was in final preparation, there came the splendid news that London had won its passionate and energetic bid to stage the 2012 Olympics. Writing this book as we are in 2005, it occurred to us that looking ahead to the seven years between now and 2012 might be a good foundation on which to base an analysis of the kind of future trends that are likely to affect the customer loyalty business during the next seven years.

Looking ahead fewer years than those seven is not perhaps very useful from a practical point; looking ahead much more than seven years would probably turn out to be unrealistic. And so, as far as this chapter about the future of the customer loyalty is concerned, we focus in this final chapter on the years between now and the London Olympics of 2012—years which will, of course, pass much more quickly than we think, until the Olympic Games of 2012 themselves become a memory.

In the meantime, what big changes are likely to happen on the customer loyalty front between now and then?

At a major conference on customer management held in London in May 2005, several speakers gave their own views about likely future developments in customer loyalty. Some of the most interesting comments about key future developments were as follows.

Increasing importance of women as customers

At present, about 70 percent of retail customers are women, with the same figure—70 percent—of online banking being done by women. However, about 80 percent of customer management system design is undertaken by men. There seems to be a general perception that women are likely to become even more significant as customers in the future than they are at present, and that not enough acknowledgment of this fact is currently made when customer management systems are developed.

Increasing importance of older customers

At present in the United Kingdom, about 75 percent of the country's wealth is owned by people aged 65 or over. This trend is set to continue and intensify. There seems little doubt that accommodation for the increasing importance of the wealth of the elderly will need to be made increasingly in how organizations approach winning customer loyalty.

Increasing importance of cause-related marketing

There is significant evidence that people are increasingly likely to buy products linked to a cause they care about or believe in. This particular aspect of customer behavior seems to vindicate our own belief that ethical and moral issues are becoming more and more important and are significant in how they influence customers' buying decisions. It does indeed seem that in a society where people see fewer and fewer examples of strong pressures to enforce traditional, objective moralities, people are likely to try to find security and solace in their own moral beliefs and moral worlds.

Increasing importance of one-person households

Whatever one thinks about the increasing proliferation of one-person households and the increasing fragmentation of society, there is little doubt that these trends are continuing. It is estimated that western cities, for example, are heading for a situation where about 60 percent of households contain just one person. The consequences for organizations selling to these customers seem clear: personalization and individualization are going to be more and more important. Just because organizations have to deal with tens of thousands or even millions of customers cannot be regarded as an excuse for failing to pay careful personal attention to each customer. This point is linked to the next.

Increased emphasis on individual delivery of service

One of the fascinating ironies about modern life is that more and more we seek mass-market products that give us the facility to be individuals. Indeed, the entire history of many branches of technology is actually about increasing opportunities for individualization rather than decreasing them.

The computer is a case in point. It was initially a cumbersome device designed to perform abstract and complex mathematical calculations requiring a heavy input of arithmetic. Today, when computers fit on desktops, or even in pockets, and may only cost about the price of a family's grocery shopping, only professional specialists consistently use computers to undertake calculations.

Most of us use computers for very different reasons; exploiting the enormous facility computers have for running a wide range of applications on which we can write our websites, play computer games, create our favorite selection of music, paste a digitized version of a family photograph album, write our memoirs, an account of the first six months of our baby, or to write our novel to beat J. K. Rowling at her own game. In other words, the more advanced technology becomes the more it appears to lend itself to personalized applications.

The implications of this for the customer loyalty fraternity are profound, but they don't only extend to product brands or service brands with a strong technological element. They seem to affect all types of product brands and especially service brands; holidays put together for the individual on a customized basis, food products strongly differentiated by certain criteria such as organic, health, luxury quality, and so on. There is actually evidence that mass-market advertising is significantly less effective now than it was even in the last few years of the twentieth century. If this is indeed so (of course the effectiveness of advertising is something that it is difficult to prove statistically and easier to glean on a more impressionistic basis) then we can expect that mass-market promotion in the future will be more successful if it focuses on individualized formats (especially in areas that lend themselves to service brands) where marketing is more likely to be by word of mouth rather than by advertising.

Many of the key trends in customer loyalty today were well summarized by a speaker at the conference who remarked that today was not a particularly good time to be a product manager, but it was certainly a great time to be a customer manager.

The need to find customers who value what you do

In the future, successful marketing to customers won't be a question of creating "obedient" customers but rather a matter of finding customers who value what you do. This may be achievable through focusing on different areas of customer interests or on particular segments of customers where the individual segment might lend itself to the creation of a kind of "club"—focused around the branding—to which customers are proud to belong. The example of the travel and financial services company Saga obviously springs to mind in this respect.

The ever-increasing importance of winning more promoters and reducing the number of detractors

The legendary Frederick Reichheld, who spoke at the conference on his favorite themes of how organizations can become loyalty leaders, firmly believes that the future of customer loyalty will be about organizations winning more and more promoters and shedding more and more detractors. As Reichheld pointed out, Dell Computing has estimated that 60 percent of its customers are promoters and that Dell gets 25 percent of its new customers by word of mouth. (Reichheld also pointed out, incidentally, that because Dell knows the value each customer has to it, Dell can actually calculate the value of word of mouth to the company.) Reichheld also pointed out that in his view, 15 percent of Dell's customers are detractors, and if Dell could cut this number by half it should be worth an extra $150 million to Dell per year in revenue.

The increasing role of self-service in customer loyalty

Helping customers help themselves is a relatively old idea, and one that has become a growing business priority. Organizations have long focused on enabling users to help themselves via technological intermediaries, from the first mechanized vending machines of the 1880s through to ATMs, the growth of the World Wide Web and all the voice-activated customer management systems available today. Self-service as a model and a market has been gaining momentum in all areas where it is practical, and of course the very concept of self-service harmonizes with the growing importance of individual choice and individualism in customer loyalty.

Self-service is most effective when there are benefits both for users and for the organization supplying the service to users. A recent survey has shown that in the United States about 40 percent of airline passengers now make use of self-service kiosks when they obtain their boarding passes for flights. More and more organizations are seeking to deflect calls to their websites, although this is by no means at present always a successful strategy, as many websites are notoriously bad at interactive communication, leaving customers stuck to know what to do if their particular need is not readily available as a website option. Another problem with website interaction for anything other than merely obtaining information can be that website responses do not usually give a suitable level of "closure" on a particular need or problem, whereas a successful telephone conversation with a helpful agent who understands the need to be helpful can give closure very successfully.

For example, a customer who is concerned that a particular enquiry is taking longer to answer than he or she expected is unlikely to be much placated by an automatically-generated website saying something like "your order is being processed" if that was exactly what the website response was three weeks earlier. But a telephone interaction with a contact center agent that ends with the agent saying, for example, "We haven't forgotten about you, don't worry" is much more likely to offer something resembling closure. But assuming that the organization does know how to provide closure and to be truly helpful, there is no doubt that self-service can be an increasingly important resource for organizations wishing to maximize customer loyalty. Certainly, self-service is going to be perceived as a benefit by more and more customers as a result of two of the trends we identified in Chapter 3. These trends are the "trust implosion" and the "permanent hurry."

The trust implosion leaves more and more customers eager to undertake their own research and their thinking without the help or advice from organizations that customers are—possibly justifiably—likely to be unwilling to trust. Such customers are prone to want to use the resources of the information age to create their "own" expertise because they believe their own expertise to be of similar or better quality than that available within many organizations. The increasing expertise that many customers have in the mortgage market is a case in point. More and more customers are surprising adept at understanding technical financial issues such as different types of interest rate, indemnity, insurance, and various penalty clauses. Self-service even allows customers to make crucial decisions about mortgages by means of electronic terminals or via the Internet, and customers are able to on occasion switch from one provider to another merely by clicking on a mouse.

Or at least they are if they want to. But of course our crucial theme here in this book has been that customers are likely not to be disloyal if they have an emotional reason—and ideally all of the eight LBE emotional reasons—for remaining loyal. The message seems to be that organizations should offer self-service facilities because more and more customers are likely to appreciate them, but they need to integrate into their self-service facilities as many of the LBEs as they possibly can.

In practice, interactions over the Internet or via any self-service system will, by their very nature, be less personal than face-to-face contact and telephone contact. However, there is still scope for building the precepts governing the LBEs into the self-service inter-action, though doing so is likely to require specialized assistance and guidance.

The increasing need to recapture the personalized service of the past

Consumers today—and consumers between now and 2012—are likely to have access to a greater range of electronic shopping resources than has ever been the case before. But the information age, while in many respects making life more interesting by providing a wider variety of activities to fill leisure hours and giving people far more control over their environment, has also created societies that feature a great deal of social fragmentation and alienation.

There is no doubt at all that a major consequence of this increased alienation is the fact that customers are likely to be more and more appreciative of sincere and authentic personalization of service.

But the personalization does have to be sincere and authentic. Delivering the LBEs isn't some sort of confidence trick, but a process that allows authentic personalized connection to be made between a contact center agent, or a customer service staff member, and a customer. A contact center agent who imagines that he or she is offering a personal service by being very informal and chatty with a customer who doesn't particularly want the agent to be chatty and informal, is not doing any service to the customer or to his or her organization.

It obviously isn't easy for organizations to win this level of personal contact with their customers because customers are likely to resent too intrusive an approach to their lives from an organization until they know the organization and believe that it likes them and cares about them.

All the same, personalization is what really matters. In the days when staff at Martins Bank described their customers in the not always flattering ways they did, it was at least the case that customers expected vendors and service providers to be familiar with their likes and dislikes. In a society where only about five percent of people had any real spending power, this personalization was obviously far easier than it is today, when practically everybody but about ten percent of the population has some real spending power.

Not surprisingly, under the circumstances, there was a period when the need to understand this significant majority of the population exceeded the ability of technology to deliver that understanding. And so you got the rise of many tools organizations used for trying to understand their broad marketplace; tools which were blunt instruments indeed. It was assumed, in particular, that customers' demographic characteristics—age, sex, earnings, and so on—could help decipher the mystery of the mass market. In fact, this way of analyzing customers' needs has rarely delivered a loyal customer base on service—we are individual people and not likely to be understood merely because we belong to a certain demographic group.

Such naïve and even crude analysis was replaced by neighborhood analysis and identification of social groups such as Stanford University's "belongers," "actualizers," or "strugglers," or even the Benton & Bowles' advertising agency's psychometric categorization of housewives as, among others, "outgoing," "optimistic," "apathetic," "indifferent," or "contented."

The mass market is disintegrating. What will be important to future service businesses is joining up the information they already have about customers' relationship preferences and responding and rewarding them appropriately. Currently CRM systems are intended to track the patterns and habits of various market segments in detail— but this information rarely supports a service provider engaged in a meaningful live conversation.

We would suggest that every time a customer makes contact, learn something new about him or her. Research should develop revealing questions to ask at the end of customer-care calls. If you put those questions to use every time you contact a customer, you'll understand him or her more and increase your ability to build a relationship. Some organizations are using information about how their customers live and then thanking them in ways that are tailored for their lives.

One telephone service provider in Boston, Massachusetts, improved its customer loyalty by nearly 12 percent through one simple pro-gram. The provider asked customers what dry cleaners they used, tracked down the most popular dry cleaners in their areas and gave customers discount cards for their nearest dry cleaner. The concept didn't even take much time or money. The discount cards weren't expensive because the only cost incurred was for printing. Other than that, the provider simply had to contact several dry cleaners to arrange discounts. But the perceived value to the customer was high. As a result, the provider reaped bountiful customer loyalty. Every time a customer used the card, he or she saw the service provider's logo—a subtle reminder the carrier appreciated his or her business.

Increasing difficulty of making unsolicited sales to customers

We live in a digital age and we can be confident that the years between now and 2012 are likely to be even more digital in their nature in the future. It follows that organizations have little choice but to meet this communications preference and to deliver a service that exploits the opportunities furnished by digital technology. The inventiveness that organizations bring to this task will be a major defining factor in their success. Closely related—and indeed part of—the digital era in which we are living is the fact that customers are more and more choosy, and even dictating the way they receive communications. In practice this makes it increasingly difficult for organizations to make unsolicited approaches to customers. The challenges this poses for organizations are going to become more and more a factor in defining success in the future.

Increasing opportunities for organizations to exploit customer desire to "belong" to organizations with an excellent reputation

In a society that is fragmented and where people feel increasingly alienated, people want friends more and more. Organizations need to recognize this, and to recognize at the same time the powerful poten-tial there is for giving customers the privileged sense of belonging to an organization with an excellent reputation. The conscious decision to create a community of members—that is customers—is one which most organizations are only just starting to understand should be at the heart of their marketing policy and at the core of their initiative to win customer loyalty.

By the way, never stop making a fuss over your loyal customers. Reserve your very best deals for them, not for the new customers you are wooing. Remember that it is your regular and loyal customers who, most of all, can make you rich.

Never let the honeymoon end. After all, why should it?

The need to make the most of existing customers

The information age has led to customers having a pretty free choice in terms of what marketing information they receive. In principle, the full utilization of suitable IT systems should allow organizations to target specific offers at existing customers, but in practice most organizations make much too little of their existing customers and do not have sufficient coherent information about them. Organizations often do have vast amounts of information but no intelligent way of sharing or using it.

Furthermore, with more and more people registering for the Telephone Preference Service (TPS) the future of cold calling has to be on its way out. There is a curious dynamic at the heart of the customer mentality whereby people do want more and more to see their preferred suppliers as friends, but also are increasingly suspicious of what they perceive as blanket impositions on their freedom.

But there is not really a contradiction here; all that is happening is that human beings are expressing their wish *to live within a friendly community while excluding strangers and people they don't trust*. And if you want to explore the days when that wish first manifested itself, you need to travel back in time much, much farther than to any of the previous times discussed so far in *Customer Loyalty: a guide for time travelers*. You need to journey back to the infancy not of the modern consumer economy, but to the childhood of our species.

10 Summary of key points

The following is a summary of the major points made in *Customer Loyalty: a guide for time travelers*:

- Customers are placing increasing emphasis on the way they are treated. If you want to keep your customers, you have to make sure they feel impressed with your organization, not just "OK."
- There is clear evidence that even in today's society and market-places which feature a multiplicity of choice, customers do in fact want to be loyal.
- A service business sells itself and when it does this successfully, it *makes friends* with its customers.
- The feelings a service organization should aim to generate in its customers are very akin to what a good friendship delivers—feeling important and individual, a sense of being listened to, knowing who you can trust, and who will have time for a useful chat.
- Customer thinking runs something like this: if we have found a service brand that we can make friends with, why on earth would we want to shop around?
- Too many organizations have forgotten—or not bothered to learn—that customers do in fact want to be loyal.
- Winning customers and keeping them coming back are the most hard-fought elements of modern business.
- Merely satisfying customers isn't enough to win their loyalty.
- If organizations want to win customer loyalty they need to impress customers.
- Today is the age of the service brand, just as the nineteenth century was the age of the product brand.
- When an organization sells a service brand, it is really selling itself.
- Today's customer needs are substantially shaped by particular social trends and especially by:

- interconnected individualism
- the permanent hurry
- the trust implosion
- ethic-quette
- rude rage
- stressfulness of choice
- authenticity addiction.

- Winning customer loyalty brings clear provable financial benefits to organizations.
- Frederick Reichheld's "one question that really matters" is: "would you recommend this organization to a friend, relative, or colleague?"
- Reichheld's research has revealed undeniable evidence that only a strongly affirmative response to this question counts as constituting customer loyalty. People who do make this strongly affirmative response can be described as "promoters" and are extremely valuable assets for any organization.

Cape Consulting has identified eight loyalty-building experiences (LBEs) that are crucial to the process of building loyalty between a customer and an organization.

These LBEs are as follows:

- LBE 1: "It's easy to access someone who can help."
- LBE 2: "I spoke to a person who appeared/sounded positive and eager to help."
- LBE 3: "The person I spoke to listened well to what I had to say."
- LBE 4: "I felt I had enough time and did not feel rushed."
- LBE 5: "I got a chance to ask any questions I had."
- LBE 6: "The person I spoke to seemed to have a good knowledge of what he/she was talking about."
- LBE 7: "The person I spoke to at the organization really gave the impression that he/she enjoyed speaking to me."
- LBE 8: "The interaction was concluded to my complete satisfaction."

Bibliography

B&CE (2002) Benefit Schemes Research, Edition 3, June, reported on www.orc.co.uk.

Beeton, Isabella (1861) *The Book of Household Management*, London: Ward, Lock.

Bell, C. R. and Zemke, R. E. (1987) "Service breakdown: the road to recovery," *Management Review*, October, pp. 32–5.

Berry, L. L. (1995) *On Great Service*, New York: Free Press.

Covey, Stephen (1989) *The Seven Habits of Highly Effective People*, London: Free Press.

De Bono, Edward (2005) *The Nature Of Innovation, Part 6 – Making It Pay*, quoted on www. debono.org, March 7.

Dickens, Charles (1843) *A Christmas Carol*, London: Chapman & Hall.

Drucker, Peter (1993) *Post Capitalist Society*, London: Harper Business.

Friedman, William (1990) *About Time: Inventing the fourth dimension*, Boston, Mass.: MIT Press.

Galsworthy, John (2002) *The Forsyte Saga Volume 1* (*The Man of Property, In Chancery* and *To Let*) London: Wordsworth.

Gleick, James (2000) *Faster: The acceleration of just about everything*, New York: Vintage.

Harris (2005) "Fewer Americans than Europeans have trust in the media – press, radio and TV," *The Harris Poll* No. 4, January 13 (online) www.harris interactive.com/harris_poll/index.asp?PID=534.

Heskett, J. L., Sasser Jr, W. E., and Schlesinger, L, A. (1997) *The Service Profit Chain: How leading companies link profit to loyalty, satisfaction and value*. New York: Free Press.

Hill, Sam (2002) *60 Trends in 60 Minutes*, Chichester: Wiley.

Jones, Thomas O. and Sasser, W. Earl Jr. (1995) "Why satisfied customers defect," *Harvard Business Review*, Nov–Dec.

Lewis, David and Bridger, Darren (2001) *The Soul of the New Consumer*, London: Nicholas Brealey.

Management Issues News (2004) "Consumer backlash offsets offshoring," (online) www.management-issues.com/display_page.asp?section: research&id=1281, May 12.

Maslow, A. H. (1943) "A theory of human motivation," *Psychological Review*, Vol. 50, pp. 370–96.

Bibliography

Maslow, A. (1954) *Motivation and personality*, New York: Harper.

Michalos, Alex (1986) "Job satisfaction, marital satisfaction and the quality of life," in E. M. Andrews (ed.), *Research on the Quality of Life*, Ann Arbor, Mich.: Institute for Social Research.

Pease, Allan and Pease, Barbara (2001) *Why Men Don't Listen and Women Can't Read Maps: How we're different and what to do about it*, London: Orion.

Public Agenda (2002) *Aggravating Circumstances: A status report on rudeness in America*, study for Pew Charitable Trusts (online) www.publicagenda.org, April 3.

Reichheld, Frederick (1996) *The Loyalty Effect*, Boston, Mass.: Harvard Business School Press.

Reichheld, Frederick (2001) *Loyalty Rules! How today's leaders build lasting relationships*, Boston, Mass.: Harvard Business School Press.

Ridderstrale, Jonas and Nordstrom, Kjell (2005) *Karaoke Capitalism: Managing for mankind*, London: FT Prentice Hall.

Schneider, Benjamin and Bowen, David E. (1999) "Understanding customer delight and outrage," *Sloan Management Review*, Vol. 41, Fall, pp. 39–43.

Schwartz, Barry (2004) *The Paradox of Choice: Why more is less*, London: Harper Collins.

TARP (2001) *Using Complaints for Quality, Service and Marketing Decisions*, White Paper, May (online) www.tarp.com

Zeithaml, V., Parasuraman, A., and Berry, L, L. (1990) *Delivering Quality Service: Balancing customer perceptions and expectations*, New York: Free Press.

Index

Norwich Union xiv, 149–57

O
Office of Fair Trading (OFT) 46
On Great Service (1995) 14

P
Paradox of Choice, The (2004) 68, 110
Pease, Barbara and Allan 129
Persil 95
Post Capitalist Society (1993) 47

R
Rank Xerox 3
RATER framework 10, 122
Reichheld, Frederich F. 115–18, 151, 152, 155, 162, 169
Rockwell, Norman 40
Rowling, J. K. 161

S
Safeway 37
Saga xi, 5–6, 74, 162
Sainsbury's 34–7, 45
SAS airline 103
Sasser Jr, W. Earl 2
Schwartz, Barry 68, 110
Service Profit Chain, The (1997) 100
service recovery 17–18

Seven Habits of Highly Effective People, The (1990) 133
Sherston, Victoria 114
Skippy peanut butter 39–40
Somerfield 46
Soul of the New Consumer, The (2001) 140
Spielberg, Steven 72
Stanford University 165
Stavropoulou, Stella 52

T
Tabasco sauce 33
TeleCheck International 75
Tesco 37, 45, 46, 54

Titanic 48, 141

U
unsolicited advocacy 4

V
Virgin 55, 141
Vodafone 46

W
Wal-Mart 51, 55
W H Smith 46
Why Men Don't Listen and Women Can't Read Maps (1998) 129
Willmott, John 149–57
Winning the Service Game (1995) 12
Worcestershire Sauce 33